Navigating Life's Tides: Embracing Change for Success

Strategies for Growth and Resilience

Maryanne L. Duan, LMFT

ISBN: 979-8-9876585-3-6

DEDICATION

I dedicate this book to my mother, my unwavering cheerleader and constant source of belief in all my endeavors. Her wisdom taught me that failures are merely steppingstones to growth. I also extend my heartfelt gratitude to my daughter, Sima, whose steadfast encouragement, and support have empowered me to reach my highest potential. To the resilient souls who have entrusted me with their stories, struggles, and triumphs in the therapy room, your courage, vulnerability, and commitment to growth have inspired the creation of Navigating Life's Tides. It reflects the collective wisdom gained from our therapeutic collaborations. My gratitude to you extends beyond words. You are the heart of this work.

May Navigating Life's Tides serve as a guide for those seeking personal growth. May it be a testament to the profound impact of therapy and the resilience of the human spirit.

With heartfelt appreciation,

Maryanne Duan

CONTENTS

ACKNOWLEDGMENTS

Navigating Life's Tides was born out of a deep passion for facilitating transformative journeys and a profound commitment to empowering individuals in their pursuit of positive change. As a therapist, my work with clients has gone beyond mere sessions. It has been a shared exploration of growth, resilience, and purpose.

The inspiration to write this book stemmed from the recognition that the valuable insights, exercises, and strategies gleaned from thousands of therapy sessions could transcend the boundaries of the counseling room. I realized that the transformative power of this information and these experiences could immensely benefit a broader audience navigating life's transitions. Thus, I intended to distill years of therapeutic work and personal growth into a comprehensive guide.

Initially, my goal was to create a comprehensive book covering the significant aspects I had recognized throughout my experience working with clients and my journey of self-discovery. However, as I delved into the first chapter, which focused on overcoming life's changes and challenges, I quickly realized that containing all the essential information within a single volume may end up with an unwieldy and overwhelming tome. To maintain clarity and accessibility for readers, I treated each chapter as a standalone book, each addressing a specific area of personal growth. This approach allows for a more focused exploration of each topic while ensuring that readers can engage with the material in a manageable and meaningful way. This decision will lead to a series of books; each offering targeted guidance and support for individuals seeking to navigate various aspects of their personal development journey.

Every individual I've had the privilege to work with has added a layer to the narrative of this book. Their stories, challenges, and the collective wisdom we've uncovered together serve as the heartbeat of Navigating Life's Tides. This book responds to the recurring themes, profound moments of realization, and the consistent resilience witnessed in the therapeutic process.

Navigating Life's Tides extends the therapeutic journey, a tool for self-reflection, and a source of inspiration drawn from real-life experiences. As you embark on this journey with me, I invite you to explore the insights and exercises within these pages. May they resonate with your experiences and guide you toward a future filled with purpose and triumph.

With gratitude for the inspiration drawn from each therapeutic encounter,

Maryanne Duan

INTRODUCTION

As I write Navigating Life's Tides, I am reminded of the impactful memories that have shaped my journey in therapy. One memory stands out - a sunny summer afternoon when Mandy, a client burdened by life's uncertainties, sought guidance. Mandy, a newly divorced mother of two young girls, struggled with the loss of her mother, her main source of support. As she shared her story, desperation and despair filled her eyes. I remember the sound of tissue paper crumpling in Katy's hands as she revealed her husband's betrayal and the heart-wrenching 25 minutes it took for 11-year-old Jenny to express her anxiety and fears about her parents' separation. These experiences resonate in the therapeutic space where the idea for this book was born.

These moments, etched vividly in my mind, have transcended the confines of the therapy room to shape the very essence of Navigating Life's Tides. These intimate stories of struggle and the courageous steps taken toward healing wove the pages of this book. From the deep exploration of self-identity to the reconstruction of one's life narrative, Navigating Life's Tides helps readers chart their own path through the labyrinth of change. The exercises and reflections interspersed throughout are more than mere words; they are a living testament to the transformative power inherent in embracing change with intention. They are an invitation to engage deeply with your own life story, to discover your resilience, and to author your own story of triumph.

In sharing these pages with you, dear reader, I extend an invitation into the heart of my own therapeutic evolution. I collected the lessons from breakthrough moments, the resilience cultivated through shared tears and laughter, and the profound joy witnessed in the triumphs of those I've worked with. All these elements have played a pivotal role in weaving the fabric of this book. May my personal connection to this material serve as a guiding light as we navigate the currents of change together.

As you journey through the pages of Navigating Life's Tides, you may encounter reflections of your own life in the stories of others. The paths to healing are multifaceted and personal, yet a universal thread connects us all—the desire to overcome adversity. The strategies and reflections in this book do not fixate on rigid outcomes but focus on fostering personal growth and self-awareness. Allow yourself the freedom to absorb the lessons at your own pace; there is profound strength in the process of becoming. Remember, as you engage with each chapter, that the act of reaching out for this book is itself a step towards renewal and hope.

Crafting the introduction to Navigating Life's Tides is a deliberate endeavor aimed at articulating a clear and compelling purpose. The book aspires to be more than a guide; it aims to be a companion on your transformative journey as you navigate life's turmoil toward self-discovery, personal growth, and resilience. This is not a passive read but an interactive exploration of self, purpose, and triumph. Through the pages of this book, we embark on a transformative journey, comparing the ever-changing nature of life to the flowing currents of a river, where you'll discover how to navigate change with intention, resilience, and a profound sense of purpose.

As we navigate the transformative journey within Navigating Life's Tides, a nuanced blend of therapeutic approaches enriches the exploration of self-exploration and resilience. At the heart of this journey lies cognitive-behavioral therapy (CBT), a practical and goal-oriented philosophy deeply rooted in the interconnection of thoughts, feelings, and behaviors. Woven seamlessly into the narrative, CBT techniques empower readers to reframe perspectives, manage stress, and cultivate a growth-oriented mindset.

Complementing CBT, the therapeutic landscape expands to embrace experiential therapy, an approach that underscores the significance of lived experiences and emotions. Through experiential exercises seamlessly integrated into the book, readers engage actively in self-reflection, unlocking insights and motivations, and promoting personal growth. This hands-on method encourages readers to explore a deeper understanding of their emotions.

Narrative therapy emerges as a guiding principle, viewing individuals as the authors of their own stories. Rooted in the power of narrative reconstruction, this approach invites readers to reshape their life stories, enabling them to find purpose and triumph amidst change and challenges. The pages of Navigating Life's Tides echo the principles of narrative therapy, urging readers to reconsider and rewrite the stories they tell themselves.

Mindfulness, another cornerstone within Navigating Life's Tides serves as the undercurrent that sustains and enriches our journey. It is the practice of bringing one's full attention to the present moment, thus permitting a higher level of awareness and acceptance of one's thoughts and feelings without judgment. Integrating mindfulness strategies into daily life is akin to adding an anchor that holds us steady amidst life's turbulent waves, empowering us to remain present and engaged, even when external circumstances are in flux.

Navigating Life's Tides highlights the transformative power of gratitude, supported by research showing its profound impact on well-being. Through practical exercises, the book encourages readers to cultivate gratitude as a habitual practice, which fosters optimism, counters negativity, and deepens a sense of happiness. This emphasis aims to enrich personal transformation journeys and solidify gratitude as an enduring, enriching habit in readers' lives.

Solution-focused therapy serves as a guiding light, directing attention towards positive outcomes and visualizing a future where concerns are minimized. Within the book, solution-focused elements guide readers toward recognizing personal triumphs and setting realistic, meaningful goals aligned with their purpose. This approach emphasizes strengths and resources, empowering readers to navigate life's currents with a forward-focused perspective.

In Navigating Life's Tides, this integration of therapeutic approaches creates a comprehensive and dynamic framework. It provides readers with a roadmap for personal growth, resilience, and purpose, inviting them to engage actively in their transformative journey.

Practical strategies and tools for building resilience, enhancing emotional intelligence, and fostering a proactive approach to change equip readers with the tools needed to navigate life's challenges effectively. Interactive exercises and personalized workbook creation encourage readers to apply insights from the book to their unique journey. By encouraging individuals to continue exploring, the book empowers them to embark on a path of self-discovery and transformation.

CHAPTER 1

Understanding Change

"When we are no longer able to change a situation, we are challenged to change ourselves."
—-- Viktor Frankl

Embarking on this transformative odyssey, we delve into the essence of existence—the relentless ebb and flow of change. Life is an ever-flowing river, winding through moments of transformation and evolution. Change, the only constant in life, propels us forward on individual and collective journeys, from the subtle transitions of seasons to the transformative phases of personal development.

In this initial chapter, we venture into the metaphorical river of life—a dynamic force shaping our journey. Like a river, life meanders through diverse landscapes, presenting twists, turns, challenges, and opportunities for transformation. At times, the river of life flows smoothly, its gentle currents carrying us along effortlessly. We bask in the sun's warmth, feeling content and at peace with the world. Yet, just as swiftly as the river can be tranquil, it can also become turbulent. Storms brew on the horizon, casting dark clouds over our path. The once-placid waters churn and rage, challenging us to navigate through the tumultuous rapids of chan

We are often confronted with uncertainty and fear in the face of change. We cling to the familiar shores of the past, hesitant to venture into the unknown depths of the future. But like a river that must continue its journey regardless of obstacles, we, too, must embrace change as an inevitable part of life's natural rhythm.

Metaphorically speaking, change acts as the sediment carried by the river, depositing new experiences and opportunities along its banks. With each passing moment, our lives constantly change, and we need to adapt to the ever-shifting landscape. As we evolve, we are shaped and molded by these currents of change. Just as the river carves valleys and shapes the land, change sculpts our character and defines our destiny. It challenges us to grow, learn, and transform into the best versions of ourselves. Though the journey may be fraught with challenges and obstacles, it is through change that we discover our true strength, resilience, and, ultimately, new opportunities and triumphs.

The river of life reminds us that change is not to be feared but embraced. It is the force that propels us forward, guiding us toward new horizons and endless possibilities. So, let us navigate the currents of change with courage and conviction, knowing that with each bend in the river lies the promise of a brighter tomorrow.

The metaphor also highlights the intricate interplay between our experiences, mirroring the way a river connects diverse landscapes along its course. Our life journey is like a river that flows through different terrains. It intertwines various phases, relationships, and challenges. This interconnectedness serves as a lens through which we can view the present moment in our entire life's narrative.

Our life journey is shaped by the people we meet, the challenges we face, and the accomplishments we achieve, like how a river's path is molded by the land it passes through. Each bend in the river represents a turning point in our lives, steering us toward new experiences and opportunities. Similarly, each twist and turn in our journey offers insights into our growth, resilience, and capacity for adaptation.

By acknowledging the interconnectedness of our experiences, we gain a deeper understanding of each moment's significance. We come to appreciate how the challenges we overcome and the relationships we cultivate contribute to the richness of our life story. This broader perspective enables us to navigate the currents of change with greater clarity and purpose, embracing the ebb and flow of life's journey with resilience and grace.

This book encourages you to let go of resistance and embark on a transformative journey where change is accepted and celebrated. The book serves as a map for your journey, a toolkit for your transformation, and your compass and vessel, guiding you through the diverse landscapes of personal and professional realms, relationships, and self-discovery. Together, we navigate the transformative currents of life, understanding that change is not a disruption but a fundamental force propelling us toward realizing our deepest aspirations.

This journey is more than a passive read; it's an interactive exploration of self, purpose, and triumph. Through the pages, venture into a personalized expedition, discovering how to navigate the currents of change with intention, resilience, and purpose. In these pages, you're not merely a spectator; you're an active participant in a transformative journey of self-discovery, purpose, and triumph. This book is your companion, guiding you through an immersive and interactive exploration that goes beyond traditional reading. Each page becomes a steppingstone, a guidepost, and an invitation to take part in a personalized expedition into the depths of your existence.

This is not a one-size-fits-all narrative; instead, it is a dynamic space where you can engage with the content on a personal level. Through thought-provoking exercises, reflective prompts, and actionable strategies, you delve into the nuances of your own life. This is your opportunity to excavate the layers of your desires, confront challenges, and illuminate the path toward your unique sense of purpose.

The interactive nature ensures the wisdom within these pages is a living entity intimately entwined with your experiences. It's an opportunity to examine, question, and reshape your perspectives, fostering a profound connection between the narrative of the book and the narrative of your life.

Establishing a mindset for navigating life's currents involves adopting the virtues embodied by a flowing river: resilience, flexibility, adaptability, and an openness to change become essential aspects of this mindset. Embracing the lyrical river metaphor encourages individuals to recognize the beauty in the journey itself, appreciating the diverse scenery and experiences that unfold as they traverse the river of life. This mindset fosters a sense of curiosity and a willingness to explore the unknown, understanding that each bend in the river holds new opportunities for growth and self-discovery.

In summary, embracing the metaphor of life as a flowing river involves recognizing the dynamic nature of our existence and appreciating the symbolism inherent in a river's continuous motion. Establishing a mindset for navigating life's currents aligns with the virtues of a flowing river, fostering resilience, adaptability, and an appreciation for the interconnected tapestry of our journeys.

Are you ready to delve into the heart of change and let transformative currents guide you toward a life filled with purpose and triumph? Together, we navigate the currents of life, embracing change not as an obstacle but as the very essence that propels us toward a well-lived life.

CHAPTER 2

Assessing Your Current Landscape

"Your vision will become clear only when you can look into your own heart. Who looks outside, dreams; who looks inside, awakes." —--- *Carl Jung*

This chapter is a tribute to self-discovery, a compass guiding you through the contours of your existence, and an empowering prelude to the transformative changes that lie ahead.

In the vast terrain of your life, each moment is a unique landscape shaped by experiences, choices, and the interplay of various elements. Understanding Your Current Landscape is a chapter dedicated to the art of introspection—an intentional exploration of the present topography of your existence. As you stand at the crossroads of your life's journey, this chapter serves as a mirror, reflecting the contours of your reality. It beckons you to pause, take stock, and engage in a thoughtful examination of the landscape that surrounds you. This section encourages you to take part in the journey of self-discovery, using reflective exercises as your compass to evaluate your current life circumstances and pinpoint critical areas of change needed.

Embarking on the profound journey of self-discovery and transformation is like setting sail on an inward expedition, navigating the intricate currents and contours of your existence. It's a conscious decision to set sail on a voyage that transcends the surface of everyday routines, inviting you to dive into the depths of your being. To set out on this journey is to acknowledge the significance of understanding where you presently stand within the intricate tapestry of your life—a landscape woven with experiences, choices, challenges, desires, and aspirations. Within these pages, you'll find tools designed to peel back the layers of your experiences, laying bare the nuances that shape your current state of being. This introspective journey enables you to identify critical areas where the call for change is apparent and resonates as a deep-seated desire. You become both a cartographer and explorer of your reality.

The path to personal evolution unfurls before you as you take the deliberate step of engaging in an authentic reflection on your current life situation. This introspective journey becomes a pivotal turning point, a compass directing you toward the doors of change, growth, and purpose. Just as a cartographer meticulously maps uncharted territories, your exploration begins with an honest assessment of the landscape that makes up your reality. The canvas upon which your story unfolds is rich with hues of joy, challenges, triumphs, and unexplored potential. The act of authentic reflection serves as a compass, guiding you through the labyrinth of your own experiences and emotions. It is a process that unveils the layers of your narrative, helping you discern the patterns, themes, and intricacies that shape the current chapter of your life.

In the following section, you will discover a series of reflective exercises, each meticulously crafted to be a lantern illuminating the path of self-discovery. These exercises serve as a mindful guide, inviting you to take a panoramic assessment of the various facets of your life. It's an opportunity to gaze upon your relationships, career, personal growth, well-being, and aspirations—a moment to acknowledge the terrain that has led you to this juncture. As you participate in these reflective exercises, the aim is not merely observation but discernment. Note the areas in your life that radiate vitality and those where discontent casts its shadow. This introspective journey is pivotal for pinpointing areas ripe for change— necessary and desired. It's an acknowledgment that embracing growth and transformation is fundamental to crafting a fulfilling life journey. This journey is a deliberate act—an investment in yourself. It's a chance to uncover hidden opportunities, foster growth in neglected areas, and align your path with a deeply resonated purpose. As you embark on this voyage of self-discovery, may these reflective exercises be your companions, lighting the way as you explore the uncharted territories within and set sail toward a life filled with meaning, growth, and purpose. Let the journey begin!

Before you continue, gather blank papers, a notebook, and colored pencils or pens for the upcoming exercises.

Reflective Exercises to Assess Your Current Life Situation

The reflective exercises presented here are not mere tasks but portals into self-awareness. Each exercise is a deliberate invitation to explore the facets of your life, providing you with a panoramic view of your current circumstances. These exercises are the equivalent of surveying the land, mapping out the peaks of fulfillment, the valleys of challenges, and the open fields of untapped potential. As you immerse yourself in the reflective exercises, envision them as tools to excavate the hidden treasures within your landscape—gems of self-awareness, revelations, and the seeds of change.

The Wheel of Life Assessment

The Wheel of Life Assessment has gained widespread use as a coaching and self-assessment tool in personal development and coaching circles. No single inventor or creator can be credited with the origin of the Wheel of Life. No single inventor or creator can be credited with the origin of the Wheel of Life. It's been used by different coaches, therapists, and practitioners over the years.

1) Create Your Wheel:

- ✓ Draw a large circle on a piece of paper, or use the one included in the book at the end of the instructions.

- ✓ Divide the circle into segments, each segment representing a specific aspect of your life. Common segments include career, relationships, health, personal growth, finance, spirituality, and leisure. Create your own segments based on your preference by adding or replacing the suggested segments.

- ✓ Label each segment by writing the corresponding aspect of your life.

2) Rate Your Satisfaction:

- ✓ Assign a rating from 1 to 10 for each segment, where 1 represents low satisfaction and 10 represents high satisfaction.

- ✓ Consider how content and fulfilled you currently feel in each area. Be honest and reflective in assigning your ratings.

3) Connect the Dots:

✓ After rating each segment, plot a dot on the imaginary line within each segment based on your assigned rating. Being closer to the outer edge of the circle indicates higher satisfaction, while being towards the center suggests lower satisfaction.

✓ Use a colored pen or pencil to connect the dots and make a shape inside the circle.

4) Reflect on the Shape:

✓ Examine the shape created by connecting the dots. Your wheel may appear balanced, resembling a smooth circle, or it may be uneven and irregular.

✓ Reflect on the overall shape of your wheel. Does it look like a well-rounded, balanced wheel, or are there areas where the shape is irregular or flat?

5) Identify Imbalances:

✓ Identify segments with lower satisfaction ratings and areas where the shape of the wheel is irregular.

✓ Consider what these imbalances might signify. Are there aspects of your life that need more attention, improvement, or focus?

6) Set Goals for Improvement:

✓ Based on your reflections, set realistic and actionable goals to improve satisfaction in the areas where you identified imbalances.

✓ Consider what changes or actions you can take to enhance your overall life satisfaction.

7) Regular Review:

✓ The Wheel of Life is a dynamic tool. Revisit and reassess your wheel to track your progress and adjust as needed.

✓ Use this reflective exercise as a continuous tool for personal growth and maintaining a balanced life.

The Wheel of Life Assessment visually represents your life satisfaction levels, helping you make informed decisions and take proactive steps towards balance and fulfillment.

Continue to the next page to complete your Wheel of Life Assessment. Feel free to add or subtract segments.

My Wheel of Life

Name of Segments	Rating from 1 to 10

Examine your completed Wheel of Life and write down your reflection on your current life.

What are the areas of your life you feel satisfied with?

What are the areas you need to improve on?

What are the actions you need to take to improve those areas?

Revisit this chart from time to time to make updates and adjustments.

Values Clarification Exercise

Values clarification, as a concept and practice, has been attributed to various psychologists and therapists who have contributed to its development. Values clarification is identifying and prioritizing your core values—those fundamental principles and beliefs that guide your choices and actions. The following Values Clarification Exercise is created based on the Values clarification process suggested in the book Values Clarification: A Handbook of Practical Strategies for Teachers and Students (Simon et al., 1972). This exercise aims to help you identify what truly matters to you and assess how your current lifestyle reflects those values. By ranking and prioritizing your values, you can make conscious decisions to bring your actions and choices into greater harmony with your authentic self. Are you ready to proceed?

Read and understand the following instructions before you move on to the next page to start your exercise.

1) Reflect on your beliefs, attitudes, and priorities.

    ✓ The reflection may involve considering past experiences, cultural influences, and personal goals that shaped your values.

2) Identify Your Core Values:

✓ Take some time to reflect on the values that resonate most with you. These could be principles such as honesty, creativity, family, adventure, compassion, or other values of personal significance. You may refer to the list of commonly held values at the end of the instructions.

✓ Write a list of the core values that matter most to you.

✓ 3) Prioritize Values:

✓ Rank your core values in order of importance. Consider which values are non-negotiable and are significant in guiding your decisions and behavior.

✓ Assign a numerical ranking to each value, with 1 being the most important and subsequent numbers indicating decreasing levels of importance.

✓ 4) Evaluate Alignment:

✓ Reflect on your current lifestyle, choices, and actions.

✓ For each core value, assess how well your current life aligns with that value. Are there areas where your actions and values are congruent, or do you notice inconsistencies?

3) Consider Changes:

✓ Contemplate how to bring your lifestyle more aligned with your prioritized core values. Consider specific actions or changes that can honor your values more authentically.

✓ Look for areas where you can adjust to better align with your values.

✓ 6) Integrate Values into Decision-Making:

✓ Use your prioritized core values as a compass when making decisions. Consider how choices align with your values to ensure they resonate with your authentic self.

4) Action Plan:

✓ Develop a concrete action plan based on your reflections. What steps can you take to integrate your core values more intentionally into your daily life?

✓ Break down these steps into actionable and realistic tasks that contribute to aligning your actions with your values.

5) Reflect on Progress:

✓ Regularly revisit your core values and the action plan you've created.

✓ Take the time to reflect on your progress, celebrate successes, and reassess if any adjustments or refinements to your plan are needed.

6) Seek Accountability and Support:

✓ Share your values and action plan with a trusted friend, family member, or mentor. Seek accountability and support in your journey toward living more aligned with your core values.

The following are some commonly held values for your reference only. Feel free to add your own if they are not in the following list.

Compassion and empathy: Understanding and sharing the feelings of others.

Cooperation: Working together with others to achieve common goals.

Equality and fairness: equal rights and opportunities for all individuals.

Freedom and autonomy: The desire for personal freedom and autonomy.

Forgiveness: Letting go of resentment, anger, or the desire for revenge towards someone wronged or hurt you.

Generosity and sharing: Being kind, giving, and willing to share one's time, resources, or possessions with others.

Gratitude: Recognizing and appreciating the positive aspects in your life.

Honesty and integrity: Acting with honesty and moral principles even when no one is watching.

Humility: Modest, unpretentious, and humble in viewing one's abilities or achievements. A lack of arrogance or pride.

Love and connection: The emotional connection and care for others.

Loyalty: Commitment to a person, group, cause, or principle.

Peace and harmony: The desire for harmony and the absence of conflict.

Respect for others: Treating others with consideration and recognizing their worth.

Responsibility: Taking ownership of one's actions and obligations.

Tolerance and open-mindedness: Acceptance of diversity and the willingness to tolerate differences.

My Values Clarification Exercise

Write 5 values you consider the most important to you and the reasons they are your top picks:

1	
2	
3	
4	
5	
Reasons:	

Reflect and write areas in your life where you can adjust better align with your values.

Reflect and write what actions you can take to integrate your core values more intentionally into your daily life. Then, write specific tasks you may do for each action. Add more in the blank area below.

ACTIONS	TASKS
1	
2	
3	
4	
5	
6	
7	

Values clarification is an ongoing process, and this worksheet serves as a tool for continual self-discovery and intentional living. Regularly revisit and revise your values as you grow and develop, ensuring they remain a meaningful guide in shaping your life choices.

The Past, Present, Future Timeline

The timeline concept is ancient, as humans have always sought to understand and organize their experiences. However, the structured application of a Past, Present, Future Timeline as a reflective and goal-setting tool gained popularity in life coaching and personal development in the latter part of the 20th century.

The Past, Present, Future Timeline is a reflective exercise designed to provide a comprehensive view of your life journey. This tool allows you to explore significant events, experiences, and aspirations across three temporal dimensions: the past, present, and future. Creating a visual representation of your timeline helps you gain insights into patterns, connections, and the evolution of your life story. This reflective exercise encourages self-awareness, goal setting, and a deeper understanding of how your past influences your present and future. This self-awareness is a powerful catalyst for meaningful change and sets the stage for intentional and purpose-driven actions.

Grab a few colored pencils, markers, or pens before you continue to the next page to complete your timeline. Read the instructions first before you start the exercise.

Past:

1) On the numbered lines, write past key events, milestones, significant achievements, challenges, or experiences from your earlier years till now, both positive and negative.

2) Write key points for success and failure on the line below the numbered line for each entry.

Present:

1) On the numbered lines, document your current situation, focusing on various aspects of your life. Include details about your relationships, career, health,

finances, personal development, and other relevant factors.

2) On the line below the numbered line for each entry, write key points for success and failure, or your level of satisfaction.

Future:

1) On the numbered lines, identify your aspirations, dreams, and goals for the future. Be specific about what you hope to achieve in various areas of your life. Consider both short-term and long-term goals.

2) On the line below the numbered line for each entry, write the strengths and challenges you might face.

3) Connect Events and Patterns:

   ✓ Using colored pencils or markers, draw connecting lines between related events or experiences across the timeline.

   ✓ Identify patterns, influences, and challenges between past events, your current situation, and your envisioned future.

My Past, Present, Future Timeline

Past Key Events Lessons/Aspirations Motivations	Present Situations Lessons/Aspirations Motivations	Future Visions Lessons/Aspirations Motivations
1		
2		
3		
4		

5		
6		
7		
8		
I was	I am	I will be

Reflect and complete the following tasks:

Write certain events or achievements in the past that have influenced your growth, choices, and perspectives over time.

Note the emotional resonance associated with each event on the timeline. Reflect on how these emotional experiences have shaped your outlook and decisions.

Set realistic and actionable goals for the future based on your future aspirations.

My goals for the next 3 years:

These are the steps I will take to reach those goals:

My goals for the next 5-10 years:

These are the steps I will take to reach those goals:

Regularly assess and reflect on the progress you've made toward these goals. What successes have you achieved, and where have you faced challenges? What adjustments do you need to make?

Strengths and Weaknesses Analysis

Each person has unique qualities that include different strengths and weaknesses. Recognizing your strengths and weaknesses is crucial for personal growth and development. Identifying your strengths lets you take advantage of your talents and abilities, which can help you succeed in various areas of life. On the other hand, acknowledging your weaknesses enables you to pinpoint areas where you can improve and develop your skills, leading to self-enhancement and personal growth. By utilizing your strengths and working on your weaknesses, you can align your actions and decisions with your goals, ultimately leading to greater self-awareness, effectiveness, and satisfaction.

In this groundbreaking book Now, Discover Your Strengths, Buckingham identified 34 strength themes (2001). Feel free to use your own if not included in the list:

Achiever: Driven by a constant need for accomplishment and the ability to set and meet goals.

Activator: Motivated to act and initiate change, often inspiring others to do the same.

Adaptability: Comfortable with uncertainty and able to adjust quickly to changing circumstances.

Analytical: Possesses a logical and systematic approach to problem-solving, seeking to understand the root causes of issues.

Arranger: Skilled at organizing people and resources efficiently to achieve desired outcomes.

Belief: Strong core values and principles that shape decisions and actions.

Command: Assertive and decisive, taking charge and leading confidently in challenging situations.

Communication: Articulate and persuasive, capable of expressing ideas clearly and effectively.

Competition: Thrives on comparison and seeks to outperform others, driving towards excellence.

Connectedness: Recognizes the interrelatedness of all things and seeks to establish meaningful connections between people and ideas.

Consistency: Values predictability and strives to maintain standards and routines to create stability.

Context: Draws insights from historical or contextual knowledge to understand the present and inform decision-making.

Deliberative: Cautious and thoughtful, take time to weigh options carefully before making decisions or acting.

Developer: Nurturing and supportive, enjoys helping others grow and reach their full potential.

Discipline: Structured and organized, thrives on routine and order to achieve goals.

Empathy: Able to understand and share the feelings of others, demonstrating compassion and support.

Focus: Capable of concentrating intensely on tasks and goals, avoiding distractions to achieve desired outcomes.

Futuristic: Inspired by vision and possibility, focuses on future-oriented goals and innovations.

Harmony: Seeks to minimize conflict and promote harmony, fostering positive relationships and collaboration.

Ideation: Creative and innovative, generates novel ideas and solutions by making unexpected connections.

Includer: Inclusive and accepting, values diversity, and ensures everyone feels welcome and valued.

Individualization: Recognizes and appreciates the unique qualities of each person, tailoring interactions, and support accordingly.

Input: Curious and knowledge-seeking, enjoys gathering information and collecting resources for future use.

Intellection: Reflective and introspective, enjoys deep thinking and analysis to understand complex ideas.

Learner: Driven by a love of learning and seeks to acquire new knowledge and skills throughout life.

Maximizer: Focuses on strengths and strives for excellence, seeking to optimize performance and outcomes.

Positivity: Optimistic and upbeat, sees the bright side of situations, and spreads enthusiasm to others.

Relator: Values deep and meaningful connections with others, building strong and trusting relationships.

Responsibility: Reliable and accountable, takes ownership of tasks and commitments seriously.

Restorative: Skilled at problem-solving and troubleshooting, adept at finding solutions to fix or repair problems.

Self-Assurance: Confident and self-assured, trusts in one's abilities and judgments.

Significance: Desire to make a meaningful impact and be recognized for contributions.

Strategic: Forward-thinking and strategic, able to anticipate future challenges and plan accordingly.

Woo (Winning Others Over): Charismatic and persuasive, enjoys building rapport and influencing others positively.

Here are some common weaknesses that individuals may face:

Procrastination: Delaying tasks or decisions can lead to missed opportunities and increased stress.

Lack of assertiveness: Difficulty expressing thoughts, needs, or desires, which may result in being taken advantage of or overlooked.

Poor time management: Struggling to prioritize tasks or allocate time effectively, leading to inefficiency and missed deadlines.

Perfectionism: Setting unrealistic standards for oneself or others, which can cause anxiety, burnout, or dissatisfaction with outcomes.

Difficulty with conflict resolution: Avoiding or mishandling conflicts can strain relationships and hinder collaboration.

Lack of delegation: Reluctance to delegate tasks or responsibilities, leading to overwhelm and reduced productivity.

Inflexibility: Resistance to change or difficulty adapting to new circumstances can impede personal and professional growth.

Overcommitment: Taking on too many obligations or responsibilities leads to stress, exhaustion, and struggling to meet expectations.

Poor communication skills: Difficulty expressing ideas clearly or listening effectively, leading to misunderstandings and ineffective collaboration.

Negative self-talk: Engaging in self-criticism or self-doubt can erode confidence and motivation.

Fear of Failure: Avoiding challenges or risks due to a fear of failure can limit opportunities for growth and success.

Lack of self-awareness: Failure to recognize strengths and weaknesses can lead to ineffective decision-making and goal setting.

Strengths and weaknesses analysis involves identifying your personal strengths and weaknesses, reflecting on how to leverage strengths, and addressing weaknesses in times of change. What are some strengths you have that have helped you in the past to navigate through challenges and changes? What areas will you need help and improvement in to navigate future changes successfully?

My Strengths and Weaknesses Analysis

Identify Strengths: List your personal strengths or qualities that contribute positively to your life and the lives of others.

How do your strengths manifest in different areas of your life, such as work, relationships, health, and personal growth?

Identify your weaknesses—areas where you feel less confident or face challenges.

How do your weaknesses manifest in different areas of your life, such as work, relationships, health, and personal growth?

Reflect on strategies to address or improve upon your weaknesses. Are there learning opportunities or areas for growth?

Who can you turn to for support or what resources you may have that can help you address your weaknesses?

Create an Action Plan for utilizing your strengths and addressing weaknesses. Set specifics.

Life Seasons Reflection

Life seasons represent symbolic stages or intervals in an individual's journey, characterized by distinct themes, challenges, and opportunities. While these seasons lack rigid timelines and vary for each person, they provide a framework for comprehending the diverse range of human experiences. Here are some commonly recognized life phases:

Season of Growth: This phase typically occurs during childhood and adolescence and is marked by learning, exploration, and personal development as individuals form their identity and values (Erikson, 1963).

Season of Exploration: Young adulthood often encompasses a period of exploration, where individuals seek to establish independence, pursue education, and explore career options (Arnett, 2000).

Season of Establishment: In midlife, individuals may enter a season focused on establishing themselves in their careers, relationships, and families, striving for stability and success (Levinson, 1978).

Season of Reflection: As individuals approach later adulthood and retirement, they may enter a reflective phase, contemplating their life's accomplishments, relationships, and legacy (Carstensen, 2006).

Season of Legacy: In the later stages of life, individuals may focus on leaving a legacy, imparting wisdom, and nurturing relationships with younger generations (Erikson, 1963).

Season of Change: The season of change encompasses significant life transitions, including leaving home for college, embarking on career changes, relocating to new places, entering marriage, and starting a family, experiencing parenthood, coping with the loss of health, or loved ones, and navigating shifts in personal relationships (Arnett, 2000; Erikson, 1959).

Empty Nest Season: As children grow and leave home, individuals may transition into the empty nest season. This period involves adapting to a new lifestyle without the presence of children, rediscovering personal interests and passions, and prioritizing self-care and individual pursuits (Erickson, 1959; Umberson et al., 2010).

Retirement Season: The retirement season signifies the transition from a career-focused life to a phase of leisure and relaxation. It presents opportunities for redefining one's sense of purpose, exploring new hobbies and interests, and enjoying the fruits of lifelong labor (Floyd et al., 2010; Wang & Shi, 2014).

Season of Wisdom: Later in life, individuals may enter a season characterized by wisdom, marked by accumulated life experiences, insights, and a deeper understanding of oneself and others. This phase often involves mentoring, sharing knowledge and wisdom with younger generations, and reflecting on one's life journey (Erikson, 1959; Roberts et al., 2009).

These life seasons serve as guideposts, offering insight into the diverse stages and transitions individuals may experience throughout their lives. The life seasons mentioned here are not linear. People can go through multiple seasons at the same time. The timing and experiences within each season can be different for everyone. Life is constantly changing, and these seasons help us understand the diverse and evolving nature of the human experience. Use the worksheet provided as a reference and modify it as necessary.

Life Seasons Reflection

Reflect and identify your current life season(s). Is it a season of growth, challenges, transition, or stability?

Is it unique to you or other people may experience this kind of season?

What lessons have you learned during your current life season? What insights have you gained, and how have you grown?

Acknowledge and reflect on any challenges faced during this season. How have these challenges shaped your character and resilience?

Based on your reflections, set intentions for how you want to navigate and experience this season.

What is your gratitude toward the current season of life? Are there positive aspects and growth opportunities it has presented?

Picture your life within the framework of the season. What does success and fulfillment look like in this season?

Identify any adjustments or changes needed in your life based on the insights gained from reflecting on your current and expected life seasons.

List action steps you are taking to adjust, or changes needed:

Failure as Learning

Failure is a natural part of the human experience, and how we react to failure demonstrates our personal growth and resilience. Failure is not the end of the road but rather a steppingstone towards personal development, resilience, and eventual success. Learning from setbacks and utilizing them as opportunities for improvement is crucial. Seeing failure as a learning experience involves consciously recalling a specific failure or setback, engaging in a reflective process, and extracting valuable lessons that contribute to personal growth.

Failure as Learning Exercise

Select a specific failure or setback that had a significant impact on you. This could relate to work, relationships, personal goals, or any other area.

Reflect on the initial emotions and feelings associated with the failure. Acknowledge any emotions and thoughts.

What lessons have you learned from the failure? What insights did you gain about yourself, others, or the situation?

Reflect on how the failure contributed to your personal growth. Did it prompt self-discovery, resilience, or a change in perspective?

Consider how the failure enhanced your resilience. Reflect on the strategies or coping mechanisms you employed to navigate through the setback.

How can you apply the lessons learned from this failure to future challenges or similar situations? How can this experience inform your decision-making?

Celebrate the growth and resilience developed in the process of overcoming failure. Acknowledge your ability to learn and adapt.

Repeat steps 1-7 above for each incident you consider a failure in your life by using blank pieces of paper or a notebook.

Identifying Comfort Zones

To identify one's comfort zone, it is essential to recognize and define the areas, situations, and activities where one feels the most at ease and familiar. These zones usually comprise routines, environments, and relationships that require little effort and provide a sense of security (Wood et al., 2009). Comfort zones can be found in various aspects of life, such as personal relationships, work, and daily routines. Recognizing these zones is crucial for self-awareness, giving valuable insights into preferences, habits, and emotional needs (Williams et al., 2011).

Stepping outside our comfort zones is crucial for personal growth and development. Being aware of our comfort zones allows us to explore new experiences and opportunities, fostering growth and acquiring new skills (Ryff et al., 2012). By venturing beyond what is familiar, we can broaden our perspectives, develop resilience, and enhance our adaptability (Seery et al., 2010).

Understanding our comfort zones also helps us make effective decisions by assessing the potential challenges and benefits associated with choices outside of our comfort zones (Rosenberg et al., 2013). Embracing discomfort builds resilience, enabling us to navigate uncertainties with confidence and intention (Pury et al., 2008). Achieving a balanced life means finding harmony between comfort and discomfort, allowing for familiarity and growth (Zawadzki et al., 2013).

Knowing our comfort zones fosters confidence and self-assurance. While comfort zones provide security, stepping outside and succeeding in unfamiliar territory enhances our self-image and empowers us with an adaptive mindset (Yeager et al., 2014). Comfort zones help us adapt, embrace new situations, and navigate uncertainties effectively (Bonanno et al., 2015). This awareness also extends to our relationships, facilitating meaningful connections and a broader understanding of diverse perspectives (Friedman et al., 2014).

The journey of self-discovery and personal development involves identifying and exploring our comfort zones. By venturing beyond what is familiar to us, we can cultivate resilience, make informed decisions, and lead lives driven by purpose (Bonanno et al., 2015).

The journey of self-discovery and personal development is ongoing. Identifying comfort zones is a crucial step in pursuing personal development. It helps navigate challenges, make informed decisions, and cultivate resilience for a fulfilling and purpose-driven life.

Identifying My Comfort Zones

My Preferences
My Habits
My Emotional Needs
My Strict Routines
Areas of Growth
Challenges of Discomfort
Benefits of Discomfort
Areas of Expansions on My Comfort Zones

Identifying Key Areas Where Change is Needed or Desired

The Key Areas of Change Assessment is a structured evaluation tool used to assess different aspects of an individual's life where change may be desired or necessary. It typically includes personal growth, career, relationships, health, finances, values, leisure, spirituality, education, and community involvement. This assessment helps individuals identify areas for improvement, set goals, and create action plans to facilitate personal development and growth. By examining these key areas comprehensively, individuals can gain clarity on their priorities and make well-informed decisions about where to focus their efforts to bring about positive change. This worksheet has been created by adapting principles from various sources on personal development and goal setting. No specific reference is available as it draws upon widely accepted practices in personal growth and assessment.

When completing your Key Areas of Change Assessment, make sure to reference the following commonly recognized domains for key areas of change.

1) Personal Growth and Development

✓ Identify areas where personal growth is desired.

✓ Reflect on past experiences and lessons learned.

✓ Set specific goals for personal development.

2) Career and Professional Development

✓ Evaluate current career satisfaction and future aspirations.

✓ Identify skills and competencies to develop.

✓ Set career-related goals and action plans.

3) Relationships and Social Connections

✓ Assess the quality of current relationships (family, friends, colleagues).

✓ Identify areas for improvement in communication and connection.

✓ Set goals for nurturing existing relationships and forming new ones.

4) Health and Well-being

✓ Evaluate physical health and wellness practices.

✓ Reflect on mental and emotional well-being.

✓ Set goals for improving overall health and self-care habits.

5) Financial Management

✓ Assess current financial situation and habits.

✓ Identify areas for saving, investing, or expense reduction.

✓ Set financial goals and create a budget plan for better financial management.

6) Personal Values and Beliefs

✓ Reflect on core values and beliefs.

✓ Evaluate alignment between values and actions.

✓ Set goals for living by personal values.

7) Leisure and Recreation

✓ Assess current leisure activities and hobbies.

✓ Identify new interests or activities to explore.

✓ Set goals for incorporating leisure and recreation into daily life.

8) Spirituality and Meaning

✓ Reflect on spiritual beliefs and practices.

✓ Assess feelings of purpose and fulfillment.

✓ Set goals for deepening spiritual connection and finding meaning in life.

9) Education and Lifelong Learning

✓ Evaluate current educational pursuits or desire for further learning.

    ✓ Identify areas of interest for personal or professional development.

    ✓ Set goals for acquiring new knowledge or skills.

10) Community and Social Impact

    ✓ Reflect on involvement in community or social causes.

    ✓ Identify opportunities for making a positive impact.

    ✓ Set goals for contributing to the community or society.

Key Areas of Change Assessment

1 Personal Growth and Development
Areas of growth desired:
Lessons from past experiences:
Growth goals:

2 Career and Professional Development
Evaluate current career satisfaction and future aspirations:
Identify skills and competencies to develop:
Career-related goals and action plans:

3 Relationships and Social Connections

Reflect on the quality of your relationships with

Family:

Friends:

Colleagues:

Romantic partner:

Areas of improvement:

Lessons from past experiences:

Goals for nurturing relationships:

4 Personal Values and Beliefs

My top 5 values:

Are my decisions consistent with my values and beliefs?

Set goals for living in alignment with my values:

5 Health and Well-being

Current assessment on

Physical health:

Mental well-being:

Overall lifestyle habits:

Areas of improvement:

Goals to improve overall health and self-care:

6 Financial Management

Reflect on current financial situation and habits:

Areas changes are desired:

Lessons from past experiences:

Set financial goals and create budget:

7 Leisure and Recreation

How I currently spend my free time:

New interest and hobbies to try:

Set goals for incorporating leisure and recreation into my life:

8 Community and Social Impact

My current involvement:

Identify opportunities for making a positive impact:

Goals for contributing to the community or society:

9 Spirituality and Meaning

My current spiritual practice:

Reflect on what spirituality means to me:

Set goals for deepening spiritual connection and finding meaning in life:

10 Education and Lifelong Learning

Evaluate current educational pursuits or desire for further learning:

What I am interested in learning:

What I need to learn for career development:

Goals for learning new knowledge or skills:

Summarizing from the above 10 exercises, what are your short-term goals?

What are your long-term goals?

This chapter is essential for our personal growth and transformation. Through introspective exercises and reflective prompts, it guides us to explore our present circumstances, values, strengths, and aspirations. By clarifying our current situation, we can act intentionally and find purpose. This chapter empowers us to navigate change with resilience and insight, aligning our path with our deepest values and aspirations. As we progress, assessing our current situation will guide us into a future filled with purpose and success.

CHAPTER 3

Setting Sail: Embracing Change with Purpose

"To exist is to change, to change is to mature, to mature is to go on creating oneself endlessly."

—--- Henri Bergson

Embracing Change with Purpose begins a transformative journey toward personal growth and intentional living. This chapter highlights the importance of developing a mindset that promotes growth and encourages readers to view challenges as opportunities for learning and personal development. By drawing on neuroplasticity and cognitive psychology concepts, the narrative explores how individuals can reshape their perspectives to navigate change with resilience and optimism. Real-life examples and stories illustrate the practical application of these principles, making complex psychological concepts accessible and relatable. This chapter aims to provide readers with a comprehensive understanding of how mindset influences change by combining narratives with psychological insights (Miao, et al.,2015). Reflective exercises and thought-provoking prompts guide readers to envision their aspirations, values, and the impact they want to have. Creating a purpose-driven vision becomes the compass for navigating the uncertainties of life, providing direction and clarity.

This chapter encourages embracing change by using the panoramic view of our current landscape as a guide. Imagine setting sail on the river of transformation with a clear vision and a purpose-driven life. Instead of seeing change as disruptive, we should consider it a catalyst for personal and collective growth. A growth mindset is positive affirmations and a fundamental shift in perceiving challenges, setbacks, and change. It's an invitation to navigate change with purpose, turning challenges into opportunities for development.

By exploring psychological principles, we can understand the concept of a growth mindset. It also helps readers understand how their thoughts and brains can change. Cognitive psychology and neuroplasticity are essential in this exploration. They show us that the human brain is adaptable and can constantly evolve. This notion goes against the idea that our minds are unchangeable. Conversely, our minds can establish novel neural connections, acquire knowledge from our experiences, and shift our perspectives.

Cognitive Psychology

Cognitive psychology studies mental processes such as perception, memory, reasoning, and problem-solving (Rahmat, 2018). It examines how individuals perceive, think, and remember information, make decisions, and solve problems (Neath et al., 2014). Carol S. Dweck used cognitive psychology principles to explore the mindset concept and its impact on achievement. Dweck discusses how individuals perceive challenges, reframe negative thoughts, enhance self-efficacy, and learn from experiences. In a growth mindset, it reveals the intricate ways in which individuals perceive and interpret challenges.

Understanding how to reshape negative thought patterns and replace them with positive, growth-oriented beliefs is a key aspect of cognitive psychology. Readers learn practical techniques to reframe challenges as opportunities for learning and development (Dweck, 2006).

This chapter emphasizes the importance of self-efficacy, which is the belief in one's ability to succeed, using concepts from cognitive psychology. By delving into methods to bolster self-efficacy, the chapter enables readers to confront change with assurance.

Neuroplasticity

In his book "The Brain That Changes Itself" published in 2007, Norman Doidge delved into neuroplasticity, underscoring the brain's capacity to restructure itself and establish fresh neural pathways. Doidge discusses how adopting a growth mindset can lead to structural changes in the brain, encouraging readers to embrace change as a neural growth and personal development catalyst.

Readers gain insights into how the brain adapts to new information and experiences. Knowing that the brain is not fixed but can develop with intentional effort encourages individuals to embrace change as a catalyst for neural growth.

Mindfulness and Neuroplasticity

Mindfulness and neuroplasticity are intertwined concepts that have garnered significant attention in psychological research. Neuroplasticity refers to the brain's capability to restructure and adjust by establishing novel neural connections throughout one's life. Mindfulness, on the other hand, involves paying deliberate attention to the present moment without judgment.

The relationship between mindfulness and neuroplasticity lies in how mindfulness practices can induce changes in the brain's structure and function. Research suggests that mindfulness meditation can lead to neuroplastic changes, particularly in areas associated with attention, emotion regulation, and self-awareness.

One study by Tang et al. (2015) found that participants who underwent mindfulness-based stress reduction (MBSR) training showed increased gray matter density in brain regions associated with self-referential processing, perspective-taking, and emotion regulation. The study suggests that mindfulness practice can lead to structural changes in the brain.

Holzel et al. (2011) conducted a separate investigation that revealed that individuals who underwent an 8-week mindfulness-based stress reduction program exhibited heightened gray matter density in brain regions associated with learning, memory, and emotional regulation. These changes were associated with improvements in psychological well-being and reductions in stress.

Overall, the relationship between mindfulness and neuroplasticity highlights the potential of mindfulness practices to promote brain changes that support cognitive and emotional functioning. Individuals may enhance their brain's adaptive capacity and cultivate greater well-being by engaging in regular mindfulness meditation.

The chapter delves into neuroplasticity and its connection to practices such as mindfulness. It examines how these practices can help in reshaping the brain. By engaging in mindfulness exercises, readers enhance their brain's adaptability, fostering a mindset conducive to navigating change.

Positive Psychology

Martin Seligman and Mihaly Csikszentmihalyi introduced positive psychology as a new branch that studies positive emotions, strengths, virtues, and factors contributing to a fulfilling life. It emphasizes cultivating positive emotions such as joy, gratitude, love, hope, and contentment (2000). Research in positive psychology has shown that accumulating positive emotions can build psychological resources such as resilience, optimism, and social support networks. These resources, in turn, contribute to enhanced well-being and better-coping mechanisms in the face of adversity. It concludes that experiencing positive emotions enhances subjective well-being and has numerous benefits for physical health, relationships, and overall life satisfaction (Fredrickson, 2001).

The relationship between positive psychology and positive emotions is reciprocal. Positive psychology seeks to understand the nature of positive emotions, their antecedents, and their consequences, while positive emotions serve as critical indicators of psychological well-being and are considered essential for flourishing.

Positive psychology fosters strengths and virtues that contribute to a fulfilling life. The chapter incorporates positive psychology principles to highlight the importance of cultivating positive emotions and strengths during change. Using positive psychology, readers learn to frame challenges in a positive light. This involves emphasizing opportunities for growth and focusing on strengths, enabling a more optimistic approach to change.

Identifying and leveraging individual character strengths becomes a key component. The chapter explores how recognizing and utilizing these strengths can enhance one's ability to adapt and find purpose in the face of change.

Readers who incorporate these psychological principles will understand how their thoughts, brain's ability to change, and positive qualities can develop a growth mindset. This knowledge provides a firm foundation for navigating life's challenges with purpose and resilience.

Carol S. Dweck delves into the concept of mindset and its influence on accomplishments and individual growth. Dweck (2006) introduces the idea of two mindsets: fixed and growth mindsets. In a fixed mindset, individuals believe that their abilities and intelligence are static traits, leading to anxiety about failing and a hesitancy to pursue risks. Conversely, those with a growth mindset believe they can develop their abilities through effort and perseverance, leading to greater resilience and a willingness to embrace challenges.

The following stories introduce readers to real-life examples of individuals who used a positive mindset to turn challenges into opportunities for growth and personal and professional development. These narratives serve as powerful testimonials, demonstrating that how we interpret and respond to challenges influences our lives'outcomes.

Narrative 1: Thomas Edison and the Invention of the Light Bulb

Thomas Edison encountered many setbacks while inventing the light bulb, facing thousands of failed attempts. However, he viewed each failure as a valuable lesson, famously stating, "I have not failed. I've just found 10,000 ways that won't work." Edison's persistence and unwavering belief in his ability to learn and adapt ultimately led to one of the most revolutionary inventions in history.

Narrative 2: The Resilient Math Genius

Charlene, a math professor at a prestigious university, had a stroke that paralyzed the right side of her body. She had to learn to use her left hand. Instead of seeing this as impossible, Charlene embraced personal growth and saw it as a chance to rediscover her potential. Through effort and adaptability, Charlene turned adversity into an opportunity. Now, she proudly displays her artwork at art galleries and festivals.

Narrative 3: The Student Overcoming Academic Challenges

Jonathan is a graduate school student dealing with the complexities of academia. In his first semester, he sought therapy because he felt overwhelmed by academic challenges, which led to self-doubt, anxiety, and frustration. However, our sessions focused on the principles of a growth mindset and helped Jonathan see things differently. Instead of seeing academic difficulties as fixed signs of intelligence and potential failure, Jonathan started viewing them as chances to develop new coping skills and better task management. This change improved his academic performance and built resilience and a love for learning. Jonathan's story shows how a positive attitude toward growth can enable students to use academic setbacks as opportunities for personal and intellectual development.

Narrative 4: The Career Explorer Embracing Change

Emily was a dedicated marketer who was climbing the corporate ladder. However, when she became a mother, she faced a career crossroads. Balancing work and motherhood were a struggle, so she considered her options. Emily saw this as an invitation to explore new opportunities and embraced change as a chance for career advancement. Inspired by her son, she realized motherhood was not a barrier but an opportunity. She embraced freelance writing, which offered her flexibility and fulfillment. Through this journey, Emily discovered a new career path honoring her professional aspirations and role as a mother. Her story shows the transformative potential of having an open and growth-oriented mindset when dealing with change in the professional realm.

Narrative 5: Graduate Student Juggling with Motherhood

Rebecca, a dedicated full-time graduate student, and mother of two juggling her studies with a demanding job, faced a challenge when she unexpectedly lost her job. Plunged into a whirlwind of anxiety and self-doubt, she grappled with feelings of financial insecurity and a profound sense of worthlessness. Months of tireless job hunting deepens her despair. Rather than succumb to the overwhelming tide of anxiety and fear, she embarked on a journey of self-discovery and renewal. She reignited her long-dormant love for art, enrolling in art classes to nurture her creative spirit and reconnect with her passions. She focused on her appreciation for the quality time with her loved ones, fostering cherished memories and deepening familial connections.

These narratives highlight individuals who, with a mindset focused on personal growth, transformed difficult situations into opportunities for learning and self-development. Their stories illustrate how cultivating a mindset focused on growth and resilience can lead to transformative outcomes in various aspects of life.

The book offers a toolkit with practical strategies and reflective exercises to help readers embrace change. These tools empower individuals to navigate change gracefully and resiliently, fostering a mindset that turns challenges into opportunities. The toolkit serves as a compass for those navigating life's ever-shifting terrain, guiding them in cultivating adaptability and harnessing the power of positive thinking. Each tool enhances understanding of emotions and enables effective change handling.

Reflective exercises evaluate the reader's mindset and highlight areas where adopting a growth-oriented perspective can be advantageous. These exercises are practical tools that empower individuals to participate actively in their transformative journey. By the end of the chapter, readers develop a better comprehension of the growth mindset and feel inspired to embark on their journey with determination, embracing change as a catalyst for personal growth and success. Take time with each exercise, letting reflections unfold naturally and genuinely.

Vision Board Creation

A vision board is a potent goal-setting tool, providing clarity and focus on one's aspirations. By visually representing goals through curated images and words, individuals gain a tangible reminder of their objectives, fostering motivation and concentration. Placing the board in a visible location is a constant source of encouragement. The positive visualization in creating a vision board aligns with the law of attraction concept, attracting positive energy and opportunities. The personalization and creativity in designing a vision board make goal setting engaging and self-reflective. Ultimately, a vision board can enhance self-awareness, provide a sense of accomplishment, and serve as a practical application of visualization techniques for improved goal attainment. Follow the steps to create your vision board:

1) Find a quiet place.

2) Reflect on your goals and intentions.

3) Identify what you want to manifest in areas of your life.

4) Cut out images from old magazines or newspapers that align with your intentions and goals.

5) Collect inspirational quotes.

6) Find a large piece of paper or poster board, ideally 16x20 or larger.

7) Keep arranging the image and quote cutouts on the board until you are pleased with how it looks.

8) Use paper glue to attach the images.

9) Use markers, colored pencils, and stickers to add your personal touch to the board.

10) Take a moment to reflect on your completed board and visualize yourself achieving your goals. Notice the emotions associated with your envisioned success.

11) Let it sit dry.

12) Display your vision board in a prominent place in your home or office where you can see it regularly.

13) Reflect and update your vision board frequently.

Letter to Your Future Self

The concept of a Letter to Your Future Self involves writing a message to oneself, which will be read later, often in the future. This letter allows individuals to introspect and share their thoughts, emotions, dreams, and objectives, shedding light on their current state of mind and advising or motivating them for their future selves. In the letter, one can also envision ideal outcomes for different aspects of life.

The idea of writing letters to one's future self has existed for a considerable period and has no singular creator. People have embraced this practice to reflect on themselves, set goals, and grow personally. The exact origins of this practice are unknown, it has gained significant popularity in different areas, including therapy, personal development, and education. Here is how:

1) Decide the timeframe for your future self. It could be a year, five years, or even a decade into the future.

2) Set the Scene: for your future self. Describe the age you imagine, the life circumstances, and the achievements you aspire to.

3) Reflect on Aspirations, both personal and professional. What do you hope to achieve? What experiences do you want to have?

4) Reflect on your dreams and passions. How have they evolved, and what steps are you taking to pursue them?

5) Envision the person you aim to become. Reflect on the qualities, values, and characteristics you want to embody.

6) Identify what type of relationships you will have. What are the needs and wants you desire in an intimate relationship, or in a friendship?

7) What does an ideal career look like to you? Be specific.

8) Anticipate challenges and consider how you will overcome them. What lessons do you hope to learn along the way?

9) Convey your emotions and feelings about the journey ahead. Are you excited, anxious, or hopeful?

10) Conclude the letter by expressing your love and encouragement to your future self.

11) Seal it with positive affirmations and hope.

12) Keep the letter in a safe place. Set a reminder to read it on the specified date in the future.

Values Exploration

Values are the core beliefs and principles that shape an individual's behavior, decisions, and interactions with the world. They serve as guiding lights, defining what is important to a person and influencing their priorities, attitudes, and worldview (Rokeach, 1973). Acting as a guiding principle, values guide ethical choices and uphold integrity, also significantly shaping an individual's sense of identity and self-view (Schwartz, 1992).

In relationships, shared values promote understanding and connection, while career choices often reflect personal values, leading to greater job satisfaction and fulfillment (Feather, 1995). Living in alignment with one's values enhances overall well-being by reducing stress, providing stability during challenges, and fostering a sense of purpose and fulfillment (Hitlin & Piliavin, 2004).

Values drive personal growth through self-reflection and motivate individuals to engage in community service or advocacy, contributing to a more meaningful and authentic life (Hitlin & Piliavin, 2004). Values are vital in our choices, relationships, well-being, and overall sense of meaning. They prompt us to align our actions with our beliefs, leading to a more fulfilling existence.

Refer to Values Clarification in Chapter Two for a list of commonly held values and your completed worksheet. What five values are important and guide your life's decisions? Why?

1
Reasons:
2
Reasons:
3
Reasons:
4
Reasons:
5
Reasons:

Life Timeline Chart

The concept of a life timeline, a visual representation of a person's life events arranged chronologically, has become a valuable tool for personal reflection and growth. It has been widely used across various fields, such as psychology, counseling, and personal development, to facilitate self-reflection, goal setting, and understanding one's life trajectory (Raggatt, 2006). Although the creator of life timelines is unknown, their widespread utilization emphasizes their significance as a tool for self-reflection and future planning.

Creating a life timeline offers various benefits, providing individuals with a visual depiction of their life journey. It enables reflection on significant events, milestones, and challenges, fostering a deeper understanding of personal growth and resilience (de Saint-Laurent, 2015). By identifying patterns, strengths, and areas for improvement, individuals can gain valuable insights into their development. The lifeline serves as a tangible roadmap for setting future goals, guiding planning, and fostering a sense of purpose and fulfillment (Thomas, 2003).

In short, creating a life timeline is a meaningful and reflective activity that can aid individuals in understanding their past, present, and future selves. It offers a structured approach to self-reflection and goal setting, empowering individuals to navigate their life journey with greater clarity and intentionality.

Here are step-by-step instructions to guide you through the process:

1) Gather Materials: Collect markers, colored pens, or any artistic tools you enjoy using.

2) Decide the period you want to cover in the timeline (for example: from age 5 or 10 to current age).

3) Working every 5 or 10 years as an increment, identify key life events, such as milestones, achievements, challenges, and turning points chronologically.

4) Provide a brief description of each event.

5) Enhance the timeline with colors, symbols, or drawings to represent the emotions or themes associated with each event.

6) Reflect and connect: Reflect on each event as you build your timeline. Consider how one event led to another and the overall impact on your life.

7) Highlight personal growth, lessons learned, and strengths gained through challenges.

8) Identify goals or aspirations you have for the future.

9) Find a prominent place to display it.

10) Regularly revisit your timeline, reflect on your journey, and adjust it as new events unfold.

Life Timeline Worksheet

Time Span: From age _____ to Current age _____

Age _____ to Age _____(first 5 or 10 years):

Significant Events:

_____

_____

Brief Descriptions:

_____

_____

_____

Reflection on the event:

_____

_____

_____

_____

Lessons Learned:

_____

_____

Strengths Gained:

_____

_____

Personal Growth Achieved:

_____

_____

Age _____ to Age _____ (first 5 or 10 years):

Significant Events:

_____

_____

Brief Descriptions:

_____

_____

_____

Reflection on the event:

_____

_____

_____

_____

Lessons Learned:

_____

_____

Strengths Gained:

_____

_____

Personal Growth Achieved:

_____

_____

Age _____ to Age _____ (first 5 or 10 years):

Significant Events:

_____

_____

Brief Descriptions:

_____

_____

_____

Reflection on the event:

_____

_____

_____

Lessons Learned:

_____

_____

Strengths Gained:

_____

_____

Personal Growth Achieved:

_____

_____

Age _____ to Age _____ (first 5 or 10 years):

Significant Events:

_____

_____

Brief Descriptions:

_____

_____

_____

Reflection on the event:

_____

_____

_____

Lessons Learned:

_____

_____

Strengths Gained:

_____

_____

Personal Growth Achieved:

_____

_____

Age _____ to Age _____ (first 5 or 10 years):

Significant Events:

_____

_____

Brief Descriptions:

_____

_____

_____

Reflection on the event:

_____

_____

_____

Lessons Learned:

_____

_____

Strengths Gained:

_____

_____

Personal Growth Achieved:

_____

_____

Age _____ to Age _____(first 5 or 10 years):

Significant Events:

_____

_____

Brief Descriptions:

_____

_____

_____

Reflection on the event:

_____

_____

_____

_____

Lessons Learned:

_____

_____

Strengths Gained:

_____

_____

Personal Growth Achieved:

_____

_____

Age ____ to Age ____ (first 5 or 10 years):

Significant Events:

_____

_____

Brief Descriptions:

_____

_____

_____

Reflection on the event:

_____

_____

_____

Lessons Learned:

_____

_____

Strengths Gained:

_____

_____

Personal Growth Achieved:

_____

_____

My goals or aspirations for the future:

_____

_____

_____

_____

Actions I must take:

_____

_____

_____

_____

Creating a life timeline is a dynamic process. It helps visualize your past and motivates you to shape your future.

Impact Statement

An Impact Statement serves as a concise summary of the significant outcomes or implications of a particular action, project, or initiative. One of its key functions is to summarize achievements, providing us with a clear understanding of the positive results generated by a specific endeavor.

Crafting an impact statement offers clarity, motivation, and a guiding force for aligning daily activities with overarching goals and values. It is a powerful decision-making tool, ensuring actions contribute to positive change, fostering resilience, effective communication, and inspiring others. Writing an impact statement promotes self-awareness, prompting reflection on core values and desired impacts. This dynamic tool evolves with changing aspirations and values, ultimately shaping decisions to leave a meaningful and lasting impact on individual lives and the world.

Impact Statement Exercise

What is this statement for (Project/Initiative/task)?

Who is this addressed to:

What are the key accomplishments of this project/initiative/task?

What are the benefits or positive influences of these accomplishments?

Identify the factors that contribute to the success of these accomplishments:

Describe the potential challenges:

What are the lessons learned that can inform future efforts or improvements?

Additional reflection:

Write a concise and inspiring impact statement that incorporates your values, purpose, goals, and desired impact.

What steps will you take to bring your impact statement to life?

Role Models Reflection

Reflecting on role models offers numerous benefits, profoundly impacting individuals' lives in various ways. Positive role models inspire personal development, career choices, ethical behavior, and psychological well-being. Research, such as that by DuBois et al. (2002), underscores the correlation between exposure to supportive role models and higher self-esteem, life satisfaction, and improved mental health outcomes. First, role models serve as sources of inspiration, motivating individuals to pursue excellence and goals with determination. Second, by examining role models' qualities and achievements, individuals gain valuable guidance for personal and professional development, aiding them in navigating challenges and making informed decisions. Third, this reflection can clarify goals, helping individuals identify aspirations and chart a clearer vision for their future. It fosters greater self-awareness, enabling individuals to identify values, strengths, and areas for growth. Finally, reflecting on role models empowers individuals by highlighting the potential for success and fulfillment, instilling confidence, and belief in their ability to reach their dreams.

Role Model Reflection Exercise

Identify three individuals who inspire you due to their impact and purposeful lives:

1
2
3

What are their qualities and contributions that resonate with you?

How can you incorporate these elements into your own purpose-driven journey?

Strengths, weaknesses, and Passions Inventory

Identifying and understanding individual strengths is a foundational aspect of personal development that can have far-reaching implications across different domains of life. Research and literature in psychology and self-help consistently emphasize the importance of recognizing and leveraging one's strengths for personal and professional success (Buckingham & Clifton, 2001; Peterson & Seligman, 2004). By identifying their strengths, individuals can gain insights into their unique capabilities and talents, which can be instrumental in making career choices, pursuing educational opportunities, and excelling in various endeavors (Linley et al., 2010).

Understanding and accepting one's weaknesses is essential for fostering self-awareness and growth (Seligman, 2011). Acknowledging areas of improvement can provide individuals with valuable insights into where they may need to focus their efforts for self-improvement and development (Dweck, 2006). This heightened self-awareness enables individuals to make informed decisions, set realistic expectations, and navigate challenges more effectively in personal and professional contexts (Schwartz, 2014).

Recognizing and accepting one's weaknesses contributes to increased self-awareness. This awareness is crucial for making well-informed decisions and managing expectations. Recognizing passions fosters a sense of fulfillment, guiding individuals toward activities and pursuits that align with their genuine interests. This self-awareness enhances decision-making, boosts confidence, and encourages ongoing personal growth for a more meaningful, purpose-driven life.

Strengths, weaknesses, and Passions Inventory

Identify 5 of your strengths and how they have enhanced your life (you may reference Strengths and Weakness Analysis in Chapter 2):

1	
2	
3	
4	
5	

Acknowledge 5 areas you consider personal weaknesses and how you can work on them:

1	
2	
3	
4	
5	

Identify and check all activities that bring you joy and fulfillment. Add your own if not listed:

Movies and TV shows	Reading	Sports	Science	Scuba Diving
Outdoor activities	Writing	Photography	Dancing	Skating
DIY and crafting	Tennis	Traveling	Volunteering	Woodwork
Cooking and Baking	Sports	Technology	Collecting	Crocheting
Art and drawing	Golfing	Gardening	Nature	Skating
Fashion and Style	Cycling	Astrology	Museums	Hiking
Mindfulness/ Meditation	Music	Card games	Hunting	Knitting
Board Games/Puzzles	Fishing	Astronomy	Running	Swimming
Socializing /Networking	Skiing	Quilting	Bowling	History
Pets/Animal Care	Gaming	Wildlife	Surfing	Rock Climbing
Learning a New Language	Archaeology			

Reflect on one passion you have not explored fully and how you might incorporate it into your life?

Remember that self-discovery is a continuous journey, and your interests may evolve. Be patient, open-minded, and proactive in exploring different facets of your life to uncover the passions that bring you joy and fulfillment.

Obstacle Analysis

Obstacle analysis is vital in personal and professional development, helping individuals identify and understand barriers to goal achievement. Exploring obstacles provides individuals with valuable insights into what is holding them back. Research shows that obstacle analysis is important in psychology, organizational behavior, and self-help (Carver & Scheier, 2001; Gollwitzer & Brandstätter, 1997; Seligman, 2011). This helps individuals develop effective strategies, make better decisions, and use their resources wisely (Mintzberg, 1994; Kahneman, 2011). Engaging in obstacle analysis fosters resilience and a proactive mindset, promoting personal growth and success (Fredrickson, 2009; Snyder, 2002). Overall, obstacle analysis is a fundamental tool for overcoming challenges and achieving desired outcomes in both personal and professional life.

Obstacle Analysis

List the obstacles or challenges that you are currently facing in achieving your goals:

Describe each obstacle in detail. What specific factors or root causes contribute to its existence? Are they internal (personal factors and mindsets) or external (environmental and societal)?

What is the impact of each obstacle on your progress? How significant is its influence?

What are the possible solutions or strategies to overcome each obstacle?

Evaluate the feasibility and effectiveness of each solution. Consider the resources, time, and effort required for implementation.

What are potential risks and benefits associated with each solution?

Choose the most viable solutions for addressing each obstacle:

What are the steps and actions to take for each solution?

Regularly review your progress in implementing the action plan. Adjust your approach if necessary and continue to adapt as you make progress.

Celebrate success by acknowledging and celebrating your achievements as you overcome each obstacle. List ways you can do to celebrate your successes and accomplishments:

```
┌─────────────────────────────────────────────────────┐
│                                                     │
│                                                     │
│                                                     │
│                                                     │
│                                                     │
│                                                     │
│                                                     │
│                                                     │
└─────────────────────────────────────────────────────┘
```

Mindset Journaling

Mindset journaling is a powerful practice renowned for its numerous benefits in personal development. It encourages individuals to delve deep into their thoughts, beliefs, and attitudes, ultimately fostering self-awareness (Morin, 2018). Through this reflective process, individuals can uncover and confront limiting beliefs or negative thought patterns that might impede their progress (Duckworth, 2016).

Mindset journaling is pivotal in cultivating a growth mindset, a concept popularized by Carol Dweck (2006). Encouraging individuals to reframe challenges as opportunities for learning and growth instills in them the belief that they can develop and improve their abilities.

Mindset journaling provides a safe and cathartic space for individuals to process and manage emotions, enhancing emotional resilience (Fredrickson, 2009). This journaling aspect allows individuals to explore their feelings, navigate difficult emotions, and build stronger resilience in adversity.

Mindset journaling is a transformative tool for personal development. It empowers individuals to cultivate positivity, overcome obstacles, and continuously grow and improve (Lama, 2015). Mindset journaling provides individuals with many benefits, offering them a pathway to achieve greater self-awareness, emotional well-being, and fulfillment.

Set aside dedicated time for reflective writing and proceed to the next page for your

Mindset Journaling.

My Mindset Journaling

My recent challenges:

How do you view these challenges? Are they opportunities for growth? Are they insurmountable obstacles?

What are the potential lessons, opportunities, or skills you can gain from overcoming these challenges?

How do you redefine these challenges by adopting growth-oriented perspectives?

Cultivating an Adaptive Attitude

An adaptive attitude is essential for navigating life's challenges, enabling individuals to embrace change, maintain flexibility in adversity, and find creative solutions. Research in psychology emphasizes the significance of adaptability for personal growth and emotional well-being (Fleeson & Jayawickreme, 2015; Ong et al., 2006). Adaptive individuals experience lower stress and anxiety levels as they can better cope with unexpected situations and transitions (Bonanno, 2004). An adaptive attitude promotes continuous learning and development, as individuals are more open to new experiences and perspectives (Carver & Connor-Smith, 2010).

In a fast-changing world, adaptation is crucial for thriving in diverse environments and seizing opportunities for success (Hollenbeck & Klein, 1987). Adaptable individuals are better positioned to navigate complex challenges and capitalize on emerging trends and innovations (Meyer, 2014). Individuals can enhance their resilience and agility by cultivating an adaptive attitude, allowing them to thrive in personal and professional domains (Rutter, 2012). Therefore, fostering adaptability is essential for individuals seeking to lead fulfilling and successful lives amidst uncertainty and change.

Cultivating an Adaptive Attitude Exercise

Think about a recent challenge or obstacle you faced:

Describe how you initially reacted to the challenge. Did you resist change, or were you open to adaptation?

Consider how your attitude toward the challenge influenced the outcome.

Write down any beliefs or thoughts you have that may be limiting your adaptability.

Reflect on where these beliefs come from and how they impact your ability to adapt.

Find exceptions or evidence to dispute these beliefs. Are there alternative ways of thinking about the situation?

Replace fixed mindset beliefs with more adaptive and growth-oriented perspectives.

Are there different approaches or perspectives that might work best for you? Notice how being flexible and open to new ideas or ways of doing things impacts your overall well-being.

Who can you reach out for guidance and support during challenging times?

What areas of personal or professional development would you like to improve your adaptability?

What actions and steps you'll take to work toward these goals?

Remember

Adaptability is a skill that takes time and practice to develop.

Be kind to yourself when you are facing challenges or setbacks.

These exercises encourage self-reflection and introspection, guiding readers to recognize and reshape their mindset toward growth. The goal is to help individuals develop a more adaptive and resilient perspective when facing challenges and changes.

Through exploring the concept of a growth mindset, we have learned to view challenges as opportunities for growth and personal development. By creating a vision for a purpose-driven life, we have set our compass toward a future filled with meaning and fulfillment. Through narrative exploration and psychological insights, we understand the transformative power of embracing change with intention and resilience. As we navigate the currents of life's river, may we continue to set sail with purpose, embracing change not as an obstacle but as the very essence that propels us toward a life well-lived.

CHAPTER 4

Navigating the Rapids: Resilience in the Face of Challenges

"Life is not about waiting for the storm to pass but about learning to dance in the rain."

—--- *Vivian Greene*

Life's journey inevitably encounters challenging rapids. This segment delves into navigating these turbulent waters with resilience as our compass. Discover practical strategies to bolster yourself, remain unwavering amidst adversity, and glean wisdom from life's tumultuous currents.

Resilience is a quality that allows people to endure adversity and come out even stronger (Masten, 2001). It enables individuals to bounce back from setbacks, adapt to changing circumstances, and thrive in difficult situations (Bonanno, 2004). Resilience protects against stress and trauma, promoting mental and emotional well-being, even in the face of difficulties (Rutter, 2006). By cultivating resilience, individuals endure hardships and experience personal growth, gaining wisdom and strength from adversity (Luthar et al., 2000). Nurturing resilience enables individuals to face life's uncertainties with courage, optimism, and purpose (Fletcher & Sarkar, 2013). This proactive approach to challenges fosters empowerment and resilience, leading to greater fulfillment and success in various aspects of life (Robertson et al., 2015).

Research shows that those with higher levels of resilience are less susceptible to symptoms of anxiety, depression, and stress, even when confronted with challenging situations (Rutter, 2012). Resilient individuals demonstrate enhanced problem-solving abilities, enabling them to approach obstacles proactively and seek opportunities for growth and learning (Masten & Obradović, 2006).

Building resilience facilitates personal growth and development by fostering self-confidence, self-efficacy, and inner strength (Fletcher & Sarkar, 2013). Through overcoming obstacles, individuals gain valuable insights and emerge from adversity with newfound wisdom and resilience. Resilient individuals also exhibit healthier relationships, as they can communicate effectively, manage conflicts constructively, and support others during times of need (Luthar et al., 2000). Resilience strengthens social connections and fosters a sense of community and belonging (Ungar, 2012). By persevering in the face of challenges, staying motivated, and maintaining a focus on their objectives, resilient individuals are better equipped to achieve long-term goals and aspirations (Richardson, 2002). Building resilience is fundamental for thriving in adversity, maintaining mental well-being, fostering personal growth, and achieving success in personal and professional endeavors.

Building Resilience Amidst Life's Rapids

A resilient mindset is crucial for navigating life's challenges and setbacks effectively. Research has shown that individuals with a resilient mindset are better equipped to bounce back from adversity, maintain their well-being, and thrive in the face of difficult circumstances.

One study by Tugade and Fredrickson (2004) highlights the role of emotional resilience in coping with stress and adversity. It concludes that resilient individuals use positive emotions to recover more quickly from negative emotional experiences. Another study by Masten (2001) emphasized the importance of resilience in development, highlighting how resilient individuals can adapt positively to adversity and maintain healthy functioning. Seligman's work on learned optimism (1991) demonstrated how cultivating an optimistic explanatory style can enhance resilience, enabling individuals to interpret setbacks as temporary and specific rather than pervasive and permanent.

This worksheet will help develop a resilient mindset and learn practical strategies to stay strong during life's challenges. It is about facing challenges and developing the resilience to overcome them.

Building a Resilient Mindset Exercise

List three personal strengths that have been instrumental in overcoming challenges.

1	
2	
3	

Describe a recent incident in your life where you demonstrated resilience in the face of challenges. How did you initially react to it? What emotions did you experience?

What are some alternative ways to view the situation in a more positive way as a growth opportunity?

What are some factors that contribute to overcoming the challenges, such as a support system, coping mechanisms, or positive thoughts or habits? How can you enhance these factors?

What lessons have I learned from challenging experiences, and how have they contributed to my resilience?

Reflect on how you typically treat yourself when facing adversity. Are you self-critical or compassionate?

How can you show more kindness and understanding toward yourself during tough times?

These are the activities that bring me joy or make me feel good:

These are my relaxation techniques:

Who is in your support network? Who can you turn to for encouragement and guidance?

These are the ways I am going to strengthen my connection with my support system:

What specific actions can you take to further strengthen your resilience in the face of challenges?

Consider a situation where things didn't go as planned:

How did you adapt to unexpected changes? What was your thought process?

What skills or strategies did you use to navigate through it? How can you further develop your adaptive skills?

List three things you are grateful even during challenging times:

How does focusing on gratitude contribute to your resilience?

Positive affirmations are crucial for shaping mindset and behavior. They promote positive thinking, boost confidence and self-esteem, encourage goal achievement, reduce stress and anxiety, foster resilience, and improve overall well-being. By incorporating affirmations into daily routines, individuals can cultivate optimism, confidence, and resilience, leading to greater happiness and fulfillment.

My Positive Affirmations

Resilience is our guiding light amidst life's challenges, empowering us to grow stronger through adversity. By embracing resilience, we learn to navigate life's uncertainties with courage and adaptability. It's not just a skill but a mindset that empowers us to flourish amidst challenges, emerging from each challenge with newfound strength and wisdom. With resilience as our companion, we survive life's rapids and thrive in their midst, emerging stronger and wiser than before.

As we navigate through turbulent times, we must recognize the power within us to stay resilient and maintain our strength. These strategies serve as guiding principles, offering a roadmap for finding stability and resilience amidst life's challenges. By incorporating mindfulness, seeking support, and prioritizing self-care, we can build a firm foundation for navigating turbulent waters. Embracing flexibility, problem-solving adaptability, and maintaining perspective further fortifies our resilience. Whether it's through positive coping mechanisms, setting boundaries, or seeking professional help, these strategies empower us to meet the challenges and emerge more resilient afterward.

Mindfulness and Acceptance

Mindfulness practice offers a powerful tool for maintaining presence and stability amidst life's uncertainties. By directing our attention to the present moment, mindfulness enables us to ease feelings of overwhelm and anxiety, cultivating a state of tranquility and mental clarity. Through mindfulness, individuals can develop the capacity to acknowledge and accept the reality of their circumstances without judgment, gaining a clearer perspective and mitigating the impact of negative emotions.

Research in psychology emphasizes the advantages of mindfulness practice in promoting emotional well-being and resilience (Kabat-Zinn, 2003). By cultivating mindfulness, individuals can enhance their ability to manage stress, regulate emotions, and cultivate a greater sense of inner peace and contentment (Brown & Ryan, 2003). Engaging in mindfulness has been linked to enhancements in attentional regulation, cognitive adaptability, and overall psychological well-being (Chiesa et al., 2011).

Incorporating mindfulness practice into daily life offers a pathway to staying grounded in the present moment and navigating uncertainty with greater resilience and clarity. By embracing mindfulness, individuals can cultivate a more profound sense of awareness, acceptance, and presence, ultimately fostering greater well-being and harmony.

Mindfulness Meditation

Engage in Mindfulness Meditation, a technique that develops nonjudgmental awareness of the present moment. Dedicate yourself to a short daily session of mindfulness practice. Commit to a brief daily mindfulness practice. Reflect on its impact on your overall well-being after one week. Before making a big decision, practice mindfulness. How does it influence your decision-making process? Below are instructions for a simple mindfulness meditation exercise.

Before you start, find a quiet and comfortable room, area, or space. Wear comfortable clothes.

Posture: Sit comfortably in a chair or cross-legged on the floor. Keep your back straight but not rigid. Rest your hands on your lap or knees. If sitting on a chair, place your feet flat on the ground. If on the floor, find a comfortable cross-legged position.

Gaze: If your eyes are open, maintain a soft gaze or focus on a spot on the floor in front of you. Alternatively, you can close your eyes gently.

Breathing Awareness: Start by directing your awareness towards your breathing. Observe the innate pattern of your breath without attempting to manipulate it.

Concentrate on the sensation of breath entering and exiting your nostrils or notice the gentle movement of your chest or abdomen as you breathe.

Thought Observation: As you breathe, thoughts may arise. Instead of getting caught up in them, observe them non-judgmentally. Visualize your thoughts as clouds drifting across the sky. Recognize them and gently redirect your focus back to your breath.

Body Scan (Optional): You can do a brief body scan. As you breathe naturally, bring your awareness to different parts of your body, starting from your toes to the top of your head, or vice versa. Notice any sensations without attachment.

Anchor Point: If your mind wanders, gently redirect your focus to your breath or the present moment. You can also use an anchor word or phrase, like "peace" or "breathe," to help maintain focus.

Duration: Start with a short duration, such as 1-3 minutes, and gradually increase as you become more comfortable with the practice.

Closing: When you're ready to finish, slowly open your eyes if they are closed. Take a moment to notice how you feel.

Tips: Be patient with yourself; it's normal for the mind to wander. Consistency is key. Practice regularly to experience the full benefits. Mindfulness is about being present, so let go of expectations or judgments.

This mindfulness meditation exercise is a foundational practice, and you can explore variations or guided meditations as you become more familiar with the process. Keep in mind that mindfulness evolves gradually, so approach the practice with curiosity and receptiveness.

Seeking Support

Interconnectedness with others is a cornerstone for resilience and coping amidst life's challenges, fostering a sense of community, and belonging. Social support provides emotional validation and encouragement during change, shaping behavior and fostering positive habits while mitigating negative ones. Networks also play a vital role in conflict resolution and contribute to overall happiness by facilitating the sharing of joyful moments. Leveraging social support effectively is paramount for navigating change and offering validation, encouragement, and a profound sense of belonging during transitions. Whether reaching out to friends, family, or a support network, seeking emotional support and guidance is essential. Sharing experiences with others can offer comfort and reassurance during difficult times. By connecting with others, individuals can share burdens, gain perspective, and draw strength from the collective support of their community (Cohen, 1985).

`*Connecting with Others:* Sharing your thoughts and feelings with trusted individuals provides a sense of emotional validation. Knowing that others understand and empathize can be reassuring. Friends, family, or support groups can offer encouragement, motivating you to face challenges and persevere through difficult times. Their support becomes a powerful source of inspiration. Connecting with others going through similar changes helps create a sense of shared experience. It fosters a feeling that you are not alone in your journey, promoting camaraderie and mutual understanding.

This guidance can offer valuable insights and potential solutions to your challenges. Being part of a supportive network reinforces a sense of belonging. This connection contributes to a feeling of security and interconnectedness, helping you navigate change with a stronger foundation. Sharing your concerns and fears with loved ones can ease stress and anxiety. The reassurance and understanding they provide contribute to a more positive mindset.

Write down names and people you consider as your support.

Regular Communication: Schedule regular check-ins or calls with friends and family. Consistent communication maintains a strong support system, keeping everyone involved and updated.

Join Support Groups: Seek out support groups related to the specific change you're facing. Support groups offer a platform to connect with individuals going through similar experiences, fostering understanding and empathy.

Brainstorm support groups you can join.

Open and Honest Conversations: Share your thoughts and feelings openly with your support network. Honest communication creates a space for emotional expression and allows others to provide meaningful support.

Celebrate Achievements Together: Share your milestones and achievements with your support network. Celebrating together strengthens the bond and reinforces a positive outlook on the changes you're undergoing.

Seek Advice and Guidance: Don't hesitate to ask for advice or guidance from those who have faced similar changes. Learning from others' experiences can provide valuable insights and potential solutions to challenges.

Participate in Group Activities: Engage in group activities or outings. Shared experiences and moments of joy contribute to a sense of connection and create positive memories during times of change.

What group activities can you participate in?

Express Gratitude: Express gratitude for the support received. Acknowledging and appreciating the support reinforces the bond and encourages an ongoing culture of mutual support.

Complete the following sentences:

I am grateful for:

Self-Care

To maintain good physical and mental health, it is essential to prioritize self-care practices such as exercise, sleep, and nutrition. These practices improve physical health, enhance mental clarity, and reduce stress, providing a solid foundation for adaptability and resilience. (Biddle et al., 2000; Patel & Hu, 2008; St-Onge et al., 2016).

Regular physical activity triggers the release of endorphins, which enhance mood and alleviate pain perception (Biddle et al., 2000). Sufficient sleep is essential for cognitive function, memory retention, and emotional stability (Patel & Hu, 2008). Optimal physical and cognitive performance is supported by a well-balanced diet containing essential nutrients, contributing to overall well-being (St-Onge et al., 2016).

In addition to these practices, other self-care activities contribute significantly to overall well-being and resilience. Mindful eating involves focusing on the sensory experiences associated with eating, leading to improved satisfaction and a healthier relationship with food (Bergen-Cico et al., 2018). Staying hydrated supports various bodily functions, including digestion, circulation, and cognitive performance, all of which play a role in resilience and overall well-being (Rebar et al., 2015). Incorporating frequent breaks into daily routines aids in averting burnout and sustaining productivity and concentration levels (Vorderstrasse et al., 2015). Establishing routines provides structure and predictability, reducing feelings of uncertainty and anxiety.

Engaging in joyful activities and cultivating emotional self-awareness is crucial for managing stress and fostering adaptability (Fredrickson, 2001; Kabat-Zinn, 2003). Joyful activities provide a sense of pleasure and fulfillment, serving as outlets for self-expression and creativity (Fredrickson, 2001). Cultivating emotional self-awareness involves recognizing and understanding one's emotions, leading to healthier coping strategies and increased resilience in facing challenges (Kabat-Zinn, 2003). By consistently prioritizing these self-care practices, individuals can strengthen their resilience and gracefully navigate change.

Here are 25 self-care activities encompassing physical, mental, and emotional well-being:

1) Regular Exercise: Participate in enjoyable physical activities like walking, jogging,

yoga, or dancing.

2) Adequate Sleep: Ensure sufficient nightly rest for physical and mental rejuvenation.

3) Healthy Nutrition: Emphasize a balanced diet comprising diverse, nutrient-rich foods.

4) Mindfulness Eating: Practice mindful eating by savoring every morsel and paying attention to hunger and fullness cues.

5) Hydration: Drink enough water throughout the day to support overall health.

6) Reading for Pleasure: Set aside time to read a book or article for enjoyment.

7) Mind-Body Practices: Incorporate mind-body practices like meditation, deep breathing, or mindfulness.

8) Expressive Arts: Participate in creative pursuits like sketching, canvas painting, or crafting.

9) Social Connection: Spend time with friends, family, or loved ones to foster social connections.

10) Set Boundaries: Establish healthy boundaries to balance personal and professional life.

11) Relaxing Bath: Take a soothing bath with your favorite scents and relax.

12) Journaling: Utilize a journal to articulate your thoughts, emotions, and contemplations.

13) Listening to Music: Listen to music that uplifts your mood or brings relaxation.

14) Nature Walks: Spend time in nature by walking in a park or hiking.

15) Technology Break: Take a break from screens and disconnect from technology for a set period.

16) Yoga or Stretching: Practice yoga or stretching exercises to improve flexibility and reduce tension.

17) Laughter Therapy: Watch a comedy show or spend time with people who make you laugh.

18) Self-Reflection: Reflect on your goals, values, and aspirations to foster self-awareness.

19) Express Gratitude: Write down things you're grateful for to shift your focus to positivity.

20) Learning Something New: Explore a new hobby or skill that interests you.

21) Mindfulness Walks: Take mindful walks, focusing on your surroundings and sensations.

22) Massage: Treat yourself to a massage.

23) Digital Detox: Have a designated time for a digital detox where you step away from electronic devices.

24) Positive Affirmations: Repeat positive affirmations to cultivate a positive mindset.

25) Volunteer or Help Others: Engage in acts of kindness or volunteer work to experience a sense of purpose.

Can you think of anything you would enjoy doing for self-care?

Flexibility and Adaptability

Flexibility is the ability to adjust or change easily to new conditions or circumstances. It involves being open-minded and receptive to different ideas or approaches, as well as being able to modify plans or behaviors as needed. Flexibility means being open to change and adjusting one's approach when circumstances shift unexpectedly. It entails letting go of rigid expectations and embracing the fluidity of life. Similarly, adaptability refers to the ability to respond effectively to new situations and challenges, often by drawing upon one's skills and resources creatively.

Adaptability, on the other hand, refers to the capacity to adjust to new conditions or changes in one's environment. It involves being able to respond effectively to unexpected situations or challenges and being resilient in the face of adversity. Adaptability often involves learning from experiences and adjusting to thrive in dynamic or uncertain circumstances.

Embracing flexibility and adaptability is essential for building resilience, especially amid life's unpredictable challenges and uncertainties. Resilience, often refers to the capacity to recover from challenges, is a characteristic that enables individuals to maneuver through tough circumstances with fortitude and composure. Cultivating a resilient mindset involves weathering the storms of life and actively seeking opportunities for growth and learning from setbacks.

By embracing flexibility and adaptability, individuals can approach life's challenges with confidence and resilience. Rather than viewing obstacles as insurmountable barriers, they see them as opportunities for growth and self-discovery. This mindset shift enables individuals to navigate adversity more easily, emerging from difficult experiences more robustly and resiliently.

Flexibility and adaptability are dynamic skills that can be cultivated. Regular self-reflection and intentional efforts to enhance these qualities can contribute to personal and professional growth. By continuously challenging themselves to step outside their comfort zones and embrace new experiences, individuals can expand their capacity for resilience and thrive in the face of life's uncertainties.

Embracing flexibility and adaptability is essential for building resilience and thriving in an ever-changing world. Individuals can navigate life's challenges with grace and fortitude by cultivating these qualities, emerging more robust and resilient with each experience.

Flexibility and Adaptability Exercise

What are your initial responses to change? Do you tend to resist, embrace, or approach change with curiosity?

Consider your comfort level with uncertainty. How do you handle situations where outcomes are unclear? Are you open to navigating the unknown?

Think about 3 significant changes or challenges you've faced in the past. How did you adapt to those situations? Consider both personal and professional experiences.

1	
2	
3	

How did you adapt and learn from these experiences? What changes did you make in response to the situation?

Assess your ability to adjust plans when unexpected circumstances arise. How flexible are you in modifying strategies or goals in the face of new information?

How open are you to seeking and incorporating new perspectives? Do you actively seek out diverse viewpoints when facing challenges?

Do you see change as an opportunity for growth, or do you perceive it as a threat? How can you cultivate a more positive mindset?

Reflect on any fixed mindsets or resistance to change. Are there beliefs or attitudes that hinder your adaptability?

Explore your emotional responses to change. How do you manage stress and uncertainty? Are there coping mechanisms you utilize?

Acknowledge instances where you successfully adapted to change. What strategies were particularly effective, and how can you replicate these in future situations?

How open are you to acquiring new skills and knowledge? How does a learning mindset contribute to your adaptability?

Identify specific areas for improvement. Are there patterns of behavior or thought that hinder your adaptability? What strategies can you implement to address these areas?

My Resilient Mindset Statements

I acknowledge that change is inevitable and view it as an opportunity for growth rather than a threat.
I embrace change as a natural part of life and use it to my advantage.
I will practice self-care.
I will maintain a positive outlook and seek support from others.
I will remain open-minded and be willing to adjust plans or perspectives as circumstances evolve.
I will approach challenges with a solution-oriented mindset, focusing on finding practical ways to address them.
I will continuously seek opportunities for learning and personal development to enhance my ability to adapt to new situations.
I will practice mindfulness techniques to stay grounded in the present moment and manage stress effectively.
I can lean on friends, family, or professional networks for guidance and encouragement during times of transition.
I accept that adaptation takes time and effort and be patient with yourself as you navigate through changes.
I believe in my ability to adapt and thrive in the face of adversity.
I trust my inner strength to guide me through tough times.
I will keep a broader perspective on challenges, recognizing that setbacks are temporary and can lead to valuable insights and growth.
I can approach problems with creativity and innovation, exploring unconventional solutions when traditional methods may not suffice.

I am capable of overcoming challenges that come my way.
I choose to focus on what I can control rather than what I can't.
I know every setback is an opportunity for growth and learning.
I am resilient, and I bounce back stronger from life's difficulties.
No matter what obstacles I face. I am worthy of success, happiness, and fulfillment.
I am resilient, resourceful, and ready to face whatever comes ahead.

Positive coping strategies are vital for preserving mental and emotional well-being, particularly when confronting challenging situations. These methods empower individuals to manage stress, anxiety, and adversity effectively, resulting in favorable outcomes and inner resilience (Bolier et al., 2013). For example, consistent physical exercise has been proven to reduce stress and boost general mood by triggering the release of endorphins, which are the body's natural mood enhancers (Stathopoulou et al., 2006). Likewise, mindfulness practices like meditation and deep breathing have been linked to decreased anxiety and enhanced emotional control (Hölzel et al., 2011).

Creative expression, whether through art, music, or writing, provides individuals a therapeutic outlet to process emotions and gain insight into their experiences (Stuckey & Nobel, 2010). Seeking assistance from social networks such as friends, family, or support communities can bolster resilience through emotional validation, practical aid, and fostering a feeling of inclusion (Thoits, 2011).

By incorporating these positive coping mechanisms into their daily lives, individuals can develop adaptive responses to challenging situations, fostering personal growth and emotional well-being (Folkman & Moskowitz, 2000). Over time, these practices contribute to overall health and happiness, equipping individuals with the necessary tools to navigate life's challenges with increased ease and confidence (Masten & Obradović, 2006).

Setting Boundaries

Boundary setting involves establishing limits, guidelines, or rules to define acceptable behavior, interactions, or expectations in relationships, situations, or environments. It encompasses communicating one's needs, values, and personal space and asserting oneself to protect emotional, physical, and mental well-being (Cloud & Townsend, 1992). By recognizing and asserting personal boundaries, individuals maintain healthy and respectful relationships, ensuring that their needs and rights are honored and respected by others (Whitbourne, 2021). It entails knowing when to say "no" and when to set limits on the behavior of others to create a safe and supportive environment for oneself (Morrison, 2002).

Establishing boundaries is vital in confronting challenges since it creates explicit guidelines for our interactions with others and the way we handle our time, energy, and resources. Here's why setting boundaries is essential in the face of challenges. Boundaries help protect us from being overwhelmed by the demands and expectations of others. When facing challenges, conserving mental and emotional energy is essential for effectively coping with stress and finding solutions. Setting boundaries allows us to prioritize self-care and prevent burnout.

We can maintain focus and productivity by setting boundaries around distractions and time-wasting activities. This enables us to allocate our resources effectively towards addressing the challenge. Boundaries help us establish a sense of control over our lives. When encountering obstacles, well-defined boundaries empower us to choose and engage in behaviors consistent with our values and objectives. This enhances our problem-solving skills and enables us to approach challenges appropriately and confidently.

Establishing boundaries is essential for nurturing healthy relationships, safeguarding well-being, and upholding self-identity (Lancer, 2018). Boundaries serve as guidelines dictating acceptable behavior and communication norms, facilitating the practical expression of needs and values (Neff & Lamb, 2010). By delineating boundaries, individuals cultivate mutual respect, bolster personal empowerment, and foster emotional resilience, mitigating stress and conflicts (Hawkins et al., 2002). Learning to assert boundaries also involves mastering the art of saying "no" to activities or obligations that deplete energy or exacerbate stress, promoting self-care, and prioritizing personal needs (Van Dijk, 2012).

Boundary Setting Exercise

This worksheet will guide you through the process of identifying, establishing, and maintaining boundaries in various areas of your life.

Take a moment to reflect on your personal needs, values, and priorities.

What behaviors, actions, or situations make you feel uncomfortable or drained?

Write specific examples of times when you felt your boundaries were violated or compromised.

What boundaries do you need to set at work/school to feel respected, safe, and fulfilled?

What boundaries do you need to set in relationships to feel respected, safe, and fulfilled?

What boundaries do you need to set with your family to feel respected, safe, and fulfilled?

What boundaries do you need to set regarding your personal time and space to feel respected, safe, and fulfilled?

What are some of the boundaries you would like to communicate to others?

1
2
3
4
5

Role-play different scenarios to practice setting boundaries in challenging situations.

Communicate your boundaries clearly and respectfully using "I" statements without blaming, criticizing, or accusing others.

Example: "**I** value our friendship; **I** must get to bed by 9 pm to get enough sleep. When **I** don't get enough sleep, it affects my ability to function well the next day. Could we schedule our talks earlier in the evening or find another way to communicate during the day?"

Decide on consequences for when your boundaries are not respected. Be firm and consistent in enforcing consequences to reinforce the importance of your boundaries. Communicate consequences calmly and assertively when necessary.

Example: "I will have to hang up my phone or not pick up calls after 8:30 pm to get ready and go to bed on time to ensure I get enough sleep."

What consequences would you like to communicate to others if your boundaries listed above are not respected?

1	
2	
3	
4	
5	

Regularly review your boundaries to ensure they still serve your needs and align with your values.

Be open to adjusting boundaries as circumstances change or you gain clarity about your needs. Celebrate your progress in setting and maintaining healthy boundaries.

Fostering a Proactive Approach to Change

Adopting a proactive approach to change is essential for fostering resilience and adaptability in today's rapidly evolving world. Rather than reacting to change, individuals with a proactive mindset can anticipate and prepare for it. This proactive stance empowers individuals to take charge of their circumstances, identify growth opportunities, and address potential challenges before they arise.

A proactive approach cultivates a sense of ownership and agency, enabling individuals to shape their destinies and navigate their lives purposefully. By embracing change proactively, individuals can foster innovation, creativity, and continuous improvement in their personal and professional lives.

Research supports the benefits of a proactive approach to change. Studies have shown that individuals who take proactive steps to adapt to change are better equipped to cope with uncertainty, seize new opportunities, and achieve their goals (Fuller et al., 2012; Strauss & Parker, 2014). By embracing change proactively, individuals can enhance their resilience, develop their skills, and ultimately thrive in an ever-changing world.

Fostering a proactive approach to change is vital for staying resilient and adaptable. By taking proactive steps to prepare for and embrace change, individuals can navigate uncertainty with confidence and determination, seize new opportunities, and achieve their goals successfully.

Fostering a Proactive Approach to Change

Reflect on your current mindset towards change. Do you tend to react passively or proactively to changes in your life?

Consider past experiences where you successfully anticipated and prepared for change. What proactive steps did you take? How did it impact the outcome?

Identify any barriers or obstacles that may hinder your ability to adopt a proactive approach to change.

Define specific goals or areas of your life where you want to cultivate a proactive mindset.

1	
2	
3	

Break down these goals into actionable steps that you can take to proactively address changes or challenges.

Set realistic timelines and milestones to track your progress towards developing a proactive approach.

1	
2	
3	

Brainstorm different strategies and techniques you can use to anticipate and prepare for potential changes in your life.

Whom can you seek advice or mentorship from?

Explore resources such as books, articles, or workshops that focus on building proactive habits and mindsets.

Practice and Implementation:

1) Commit to incorporating proactive behaviors into your daily routine. Start small and gradually increase the complexity of your proactive actions.

2) Monitor your progress regularly and adjust your approach as needed. Celebrate small victories and learn from any setbacks or challenges your encounter.

3) Encourage accountability by sharing your goals and progress with a trusted friend or mentor.

Reflection and Adjustment:

1) Periodically reflect on your journey towards fostering a proactive approach to change. What strategies have been most effective? What areas still need improvement?

2) Be open to feedback and new ideas. Embrace a growth mindset that views challenges as opportunities for learning and refinement.

3) Continuously adapt and refine your proactive strategies as you navigate through different changes and transitions in your life.

4) Closing Thoughts:

Write your thoughts and insights from completing this worksheet. How do you envision applying a proactive approach to change in your life moving forward?

Set an intention to prioritize proactive behaviors and mindset shifts in your daily life, knowing that they will contribute to your overall resilience and success in the face of change.

Adaptive Problem-Solving

The Adaptive Problem-Solving approach is a proactive and solution-focused strategy that encourages individuals to confront challenges with a resilient mindset. Instead of feeling overwhelmed by circumstances beyond their control, individuals are empowered to focus on what they can manage and influence. This strategy entails decomposing intricate tasks into smaller, more feasible steps, rendering them more manageable and easier to tackle efficiently. Individuals develop a sense of agency and control over their circumstances by taking proactive measures and implementing solutions.

Research suggests adaptive problem-solving skills are essential for navigating life's challenges and promoting psychological well-being (Snyder & Lopez, 2009). Problem-solving therapy, which incorporates similar principles, has effectively treated various mental health issues (Nezu et al., 2013). Individuals who exhibit resilience, characterized by the ability to bounce back from adversity, often employ adaptive problem-solving strategies (Tugade & Fredrickson, 2004).

By completing worksheets and exercises designed to enhance adaptive problem-solving skills, individuals can cultivate resilience, creativity, and effectiveness in addressing challenges they encounter in various aspects of life.

Adaptive Problem-Solving Worksheet

Briefly describe the challenge or problem you are currently facing:

What do you think are the factors contributing to the problem?

Brainstorm and identify at least three potential solutions to address the problem.

1	
2	
3	

What are the advantages and disadvantages of each solution? Consider feasibility, potential outcomes, and alignment with your goals and values.

	Advantages	Disadvantages
1		
2		
3		

Select the solution you believe is most effective and adaptable to the situation.

Outline the steps you will take to implement your chosen solution.

1	
2	
3	
4	
5	

Reflect on the outcome, what you learned from the experience, and how you can apply these insights to future problem-solving endeavors.

Maintaining Perspective

Maintaining perspective is crucial when facing challenging times. It helps us navigate adversity with resilience and emotional balance. One effective strategy is reflecting on past challenges and the valuable lessons we learned. By reminding ourselves of our past successes, we boost our confidence and reinforce our belief in our ability to overcome current difficulties. It is important to remember that tough times are temporary and that we have the strength and resilience to overcome them.

Positive psychology research emphasizes the importance of maintaining perspective to promote psychological well-being and resilience (Folkman & Moskowitz, 2000). Studies have shown that individuals who maintain a balanced perspective during challenging situations experience less stress and greater emotional resilience (Bonanno, 2004). Engaging in gratitude exercises and directing attention towards the positive facets of life, even amidst challenges, has been associated with enhanced mental well-being (Emmons & McCullough, 2003).

This worksheet helps you cultivate and maintain perspective during challenging situations. Through reflective exercises and acknowledging your past achievements and strengths, you can develop the resilience and emotional well-being necessary to navigate life's difficulties with clarity and confidence.

Maintaining Perspective Exercise

Briefly describe the challenging situation you are facing or have recently experienced.

Identify and describe the emotions you have experienced in response to the situation.

List any negative thoughts or beliefs related to the situation. Challenge these thoughts by considering alternative perspectives or evidence against them.

Reflect on the broader context of the situation. How does it fit into your life, and what potential long-term implications does it have?

What lessons or insights have you gained from the experience? How has it contributed to your personal growth or understanding?

Are there aspects of the situation you are grateful for? Focus on positive aspects, even in challenging times.

Based on your reflections, outline actionable steps you can take to address the situation or cope with its effects more effectively.

Seeking Professional Help

If needed, seek support from mental health professionals or counselors who can provide guidance and therapeutic interventions to help navigate challenging times.

Who can you seek support from:

Gratitude Practice

Gratitude is a positive emotion characterized by recognizing and appreciating the good things, experiences, and people in one's life. It involves feeling thankful and expressing appreciation for the kindness, support, or blessings received, whether big or small. Gratitude is often accompanied by a sense of humility, joy, and contentment as individuals acknowledge the positive aspects of their lives and the contributions of others.

Nurturing a habit of gratitude entails deliberately directing attention to the positive facets of one's life and conveying thanks for the various blessings, regardless of their size or significance. By acknowledging and expressing gratitude, individuals can shift their perspective from scarcity to abundance, fostering resilience amidst adversity.

Research in positive psychology has shown the powerful effects of gratitude on psychological well-being and resilience (Emmons & McCullough, 2003). Grateful individuals experience greater happiness, optimism, and life satisfaction, even in adversity (Wood et al., 2010). Research has indicated that engaging in gratitude exercises can enhance mental well-being, such as decreased levels of depression and anxiety symptoms (Kerr et al., 2015).

Expressing gratitude can also enhance social connections and relationships, fostering a sense of appreciation and reciprocity (Algoe, 2012). By acknowledging the kindness and support of others, individuals can strengthen their social support networks, which are crucial for resilience in times of difficulty (Uchino, 2009).

In summary, cultivating gratitude is a simple yet powerful way to foster resilience amidst adversity. By focusing on the positive aspects of life and expressing appreciation for one's blessings, individuals can shift their mindset, enhance their well-being, and build the psychological resources needed to navigate life's challenges with grace and strength.

Gratitude Journaling instructions:

1) Select a dedicated journal or notebook for your gratitude practice. This can be a physical journal, a digital document, or even a specialized gratitude app.

2) Set a Routine: Decide on a regular time to journal, whether it's in the morning, before bed, or at another convenient time. Consistency is crucial in establishing this

habit.

3) Start with Date: Begin each entry with the date to track your gratitude journey over time.

4) Reflect on Your Day:

   ✓ Take a moment to reflect on your day. Consider the positive experiences, interactions, or moments that brought you joy.

   ✓ List at least three things you are grateful for. These can be big or small, from meaningful relationships and achievements to simple pleasures or moments of kindness.

   ✓ For each item on your list, be specific. Instead of a general statement, provide details highlighting why you're grateful for that thing, person or experience.

5) Share your emotions related to each gratitude entry. How did these positive aspects make you feel? Reflecting on the emotional impact enhances the depth of your practice.

6) 6. Incorporate unexpected or surprising moments of gratitude. These can be pleasant surprises, small victories, or moments that caught you off guard.

7) 7. Occasionally, challenge yourself to find gratitude in difficult situations. This can promote resilience and a positive outlook even in adversity.

8) 8. Review your entries to see patterns, themes, or shifts in your perspective over time. This self-reflection can provide insights into your evolving mindset.

9) 9. Celebrate milestones in your gratitude practice, such as reaching a certain number of entries or recognizing consistent patterns of

gratitude in your life.

While gratitude journaling is personal, you may share some entries with friends or loved ones. Sharing gratitude can strengthen connections and inspire others.

Remember, gratitude journaling is a flexible and personal practice. Adapt the worksheet on the next page to fit your style and preferences, and let it become a regular habit contributing to your overall well-being.

My Gratitude Journal

Date: _____

These are the three things I am grateful today:

1
2
3

These are the thoughts I had and emotions I felt for #1 gratitude:

These are the thoughts I had and emotions I felt for #2 gratitude:

These are the thoughts I had and emotions I felt for #3 gratitude:

What are the benefits I received from whom or what I am grateful for today?

How did practicing gratitude make you feel today?

Did you notice any changes in your mood or mindset after reflecting on what you are grateful for?

Are there any recurring themes or patterns in your gratitude entries?

Additional thoughts or observations related to your gratitude practice.

By consistently using this gratitude journal, you can cultivate a habit of focusing on the positives in your life and fostering a sense of appreciation for the things, people, and experiences that bring you joy and fulfillment.

Positive Affirmations

Daily affirmations are effective because they challenge negative thoughts and replace them with positive ones. Over time, repetitive use of affirmations helps reprogram ingrained negative thought patterns. Individuals consciously choose to speak to themselves in a positive and supportive manner by reminding themselves of their capabilities and potential, fostering a more optimistic perspective. By consistently affirming positive qualities, individuals develop self-concepts and positive beliefs about themselves aligned with those affirmations, instilling a sense of worthiness and capability. Positive affirmations often involve proclaiming desired outcomes or qualities. This aids individuals in clarifying and concentrating on their objectives, nurturing a feeling of purpose and drive to pursue them. Consistent use of positive affirmations can reshape neural pathways in the brain. Eventually, this may result in a default mindset and perspective that are more positive. Repetition of positive affirmations has the potential to alter neural pathways in the brain. Over time, this can lead to a more positive default mindset and outlook on life.

To make positive affirmations effective, choose personal statements, repeat consistently, and believe in their possibility. Integrating positive affirmations into daily routines can lead to significant shifts in the mindset. Below are examples of daily affirmations you may use as a starter. Personalize these affirmations to resonate with your own experiences and aspirations.

My Positive Affirmations

Repeat them daily to reinforce a positive and adaptable mindset:

Change is leading me to something better.

I am open to the lessons that change brings, and I grow stronger with each experience.

My positive attitude transforms challenges into steppingstones for success.

I am a master of adaptation, and I find joy in the journey of change.

Optimism is my compass, guiding me through the twists and turns of life.

I release the need for control and embrace the beauty of uncertainty.

Change is an opportunity for personal reinvention, and I welcome it wholeheartedly.

I am a resilient soul, capable of thriving in any environment.

I trust the life process, and I easily adapt to its unfolding chapters.

Every day brings new possibilities, and I approach them positively.

I am like a tree, rooted in my strength and flexible in the winds of change.

I see change as a friend, guiding me towards my highest potential.

These interactive exercises are designed to help you actively engage with the practical tools provided. Embrace them as part of your ongoing journey to navigate life's currents with intention, resilience, and a proactive mindset.

Real-life examples of resilience are powerful reminders that we can overcome adversity and succeed despite facing obstacles. Whether it is political leaders like Nelson Mandela or individuals like J. K. Rowling, Malala Yousafzai, Bethany Hamilton, or Stephen Hawking, they inspire us to persevere in the face of challenges and discover our inner strength amidst life's trials.

Nelson Mandela, who endured decades of imprisonment, became a symbol of resilience and reconciliation in his quest for social change. Despite facing immense adversity, he remained steadfast in his principles, eventually leading South Africa to democracy as its first black president. Similarly, K. Rowling transformed her struggles into literary triumphs, achieving remarkable success. J. K. Rowling faced numerous rejections and struggled with poverty and depression before succeeding in the Harry Potter series. Despite these setbacks, she pursued her passion for writing, eventually becoming one of the most successful authors of all time. Malala Yousafzai displayed an unwavering commitment to education despite facing violence. Despite being targeted by the Taliban for her advocacy of girls' education in Pakistan, she remained resolute and refused to be silenced. Her resilience and determination led to her recovery and propelled her to become a global advocate for children's rights and education, eventually earning her the Nobel Peace Prize. Surfer Bethany Hamilton refused to let a shark attack at age 13 define her, even after losing her arm. With remarkable resilience, she returned to surfing just one month after the incident and became a professional surfer, inspiring millions with her courage and determination. Stephen Hawking defied the odds by continuing his groundbreaking work in theoretical physics. Despite being confined to a wheelchair and losing the ability to speak, he made significant contributions to science and became one of the most renowned scientists of his time.

The examples of resilience showcased here offer profound insights into human capacity to overcome adversity and thrive. From individuals who have endured personal loss to those who have triumphed over seemingly insurmountable obstacles, these stories remind us of the resilience inherent in the human spirit. Through perseverance, determination, and a resilient mindset, these individuals have survived and emerged stronger and more resilient than before. Their narratives illuminate as symbols of hope and motivation, underscoring that resilience isn't exclusive to a chosen few but rather a characteristic within reach for all to foster and foster. These instances serve as a testament that we can surmount adversities and strive for a more promising tomorrow for ourselves and those around us.

Navigating the Rapids is a guiding light through the tumultuous waters of life's challenges. This chapter illuminates the path toward personal growth and triumph by delving into the strategies for staying strong amidst turbulent times and exploring real-life examples of resilience. The narratives of those who have faced challenges and come out more robust are a powerful reminder of the resilient nature of the human spirit and our ability to triumph over adversity. As we navigate our rapids, let us draw inspiration from these examples and embrace the power of resilience, knowing that with perseverance, courage, and a resilient mindset, we can navigate any obstacle that comes our way.

CHAPTER 5

Discovering Your Tributaries: Personal Triumphs

"Take pride in how far you've come. Have faith in how far you can go. But don't forget to enjoy the journey."

——- Michael Josephson

As you navigate the flow of life's river, take the time to celebrate your triumphs as tributaries—moments that shape the landscape of your journey. Engage in identifying and celebrating these triumphs, cultivating a profound sense of achievement and gratitude that forms an integral part of your evolving narrative.

Personal Triumphs is a journey into recognizing and celebrating the individual victories that shape our lives. Much like tributaries contribute to the flow of a river, these personal triumphs enrich our journey, fostering a sense of achievement and gratitude. This section encourages introspection, acknowledging the big and small milestones that contribute to the unique tapestry of our existence.

Discovering your tributaries holds paramount significance as it unfolds a journey of self-awareness and positive mindset cultivation. Individuals cultivate gratitude by acknowledging and celebrating personal triumphs, fostering mental well-being and motivation for future goals. This process enhances resilience by recognizing and overcoming challenges, improving overall well-being. Sharing our successes helps build stronger bonds and fosters a supportive atmosphere. Reflecting on past triumphs guides future choices and empowers individuals through continuous personal growth. Actively celebrating achievements boosts confidence, shapes a positive life narrative, and promotes personal fulfillment. Ultimately, discovering your tributaries becomes a cornerstone for fostering a fulfilling and joyous life journey.

Celebrating Personal Triumphs

Celebrating Personal Triumphs fosters self-esteem, motivation, and overall well-being. It reaffirms our capabilities and strengthens our self-worth, validating our efforts and encouraging continued progress towards our goals. This shift in focus from shortcomings to accomplishments enhances resilience in the face of challenges, promoting gratitude, contentment, and a deeper appreciation for life's blessings and our growth journey. Celebrating personal triumph can be a valuable tool for building self-esteem and achieving success in personal and professional contexts.

Personal triumphs encompass a variety of experiences and achievements that hold significant meaning and value for individuals, representing moments of success, growth, and fulfillment. Whether overcoming obstacles, achieving goals, or making meaningful progress toward desired outcomes, these triumphs validate one's efforts and skills, showcasing resilience, courage, and personal growth. Reflecting on past accomplishments reinforces a deep sense of achievement, boosts self-esteem, provides valuable insights into personal growth and development, and serves as a source of motivation, cultivating a resilient mindset (Emmons & McCullough, 2003). It fosters gratitude, appreciation, self-awareness, and empowerment, equipping individuals with the psychological resources to navigate life's challenges and pursue future goals confidently and determinedly. Integrating this reflective practice into our routine can lead to profound personal growth and fulfillment (Wood et al., 2010; Lyubomirsky et al., 2005).

Use the following worksheet to reflect on and celebrate your personal triumphs. Embrace a sense of achievement and gratitude as you navigate through the tributaries of your life.

Past Triumphs Reflection

List three personal triumphs or achievements that stand out in your past.

For each triumph identified, express gratitude. Consider the people, circumstances, or your own efforts that contributed to these achievements.

Identify your own strengths that contributed to your overcoming the challenges:

How did each triumph contribute to your personal growth? Did it push you beyond your comfort zone, enhance your skills, or provide valuable lessons?

How did each personal triumph influence your overall well-being? Did it contribute to a sense of happiness, fulfillment, or improved mental wellbeing?

Identify any challenges or obstacles you overcame to achieve these triumphs.

Choose a trusted friend, family member, or mentor to share your personal triumphs with.

I will choose:

Start a journal dedicated to recording your triumphs. Use the template in the next page for reference and feel free to create your own.

My Triumph Journal

My triumphant accomplishments:

What are the efforts I made in achieving this triumph?

These are the emotions I experienced:

These are the challenges I encountered:

What I did to overcome the challenges:

What are some of the small winning steps along the way?

In overcoming my challenges, I am grateful for:

What are your new goals inspired by your past triumphs?

How can your past successes guide your aspirations for the future?

Use words, images, or symbols to visually represent your personal triumphs.

Plan a personal celebration for each triumph, whether treating yourself to something enjoyable or doing quality activities with others that bring you joy. Strategies include setting aside dedicated time, sharing achievements with others, and creating meaningful rituals. By scheduling time, acknowledging accomplishments, and incorporating symbolic rituals, individuals deepen their sense of fulfillment and motivation for future endeavors.

In life's journey, facing challenges and setbacks is inevitable. Embracing setbacks as growth opportunities reframes adversity as a chance to learn and adapt. Reframing failures as learning experiences shifts our mindset from defeat to empowerment. Maintaining resilience amidst challenges requires self-care, seeking support, and cultivating a growth mindset. Through embracing setbacks, reframing failures, and employing resilience strategies, individuals navigate challenges and emerge stronger.

Cultivate a Triumph Mindset

Individuals with a triumph mindset exhibit resilience, determination, and optimism when facing obstacles or setbacks. They view challenges as temporary hurdles that can be overcome with perseverance and hard work. They maintain a positive outlook, focusing on finding solutions rather than dwelling on problems. Rooted in the belief that one can triumph over adversity, this mindset embraces failure as a catalyst for growth, learning, and eventual success. Ultimately, the triumph mindset empowers individuals to confront life's challenges with confidence, resilience, and an unwavering commitment to their objectives (Yeager & Dweck, 2012; Dweck 2006).

To cultivate a triumph mindset, maintain a positive outlook, and view negative situations as opportunities for growth. Believe in your abilities to build confidence and self-efficacy. To maintain emotional well-being, it is essential to practice self-compassion. These principles empower individuals to face life's challenges with resilience and grace.

Cultivating a Triumph Mindset Exercise

Reflect on a recent setback or challenge you faced:

```
```

Identify at least three potential opportunities for growth or learning that arose from this experience:

1	
2	
3	

Reframe this setback in a more positive light, focusing on the lessons learned and the potential for personal development:

```
```

List three achievements or successes you have experienced in the past:

1	
2	
3	

Reflect on the skills, strengths, or qualities that contributed to these successes:

How can you apply these same skills or qualities to overcome current or future challenges or setbacks?

Write down three compassionate and encouraging statements you can say to yourself in response to this setback:

1	
2	
3	

Identify one specific goal or aspiration you would like to achieve soon.

Break down this goal into smaller, manageable steps that you can take to work towards it:

Remember

Treat yourself with kindness and understanding.

in times of challenges and setbacks.

Setbacks are a natural part of the learning and growth process.

Cultivating a triumphant mindset is an ongoing process that requires practice and commitment. Use this worksheet to help you develop the skills and attitudes to navigate life's challenges with resilience and grace.

Building Confidence and Self-efficacy

Building confidence and self-efficacy is crucial for personal development and success in various aspects of life. Confidence refers to the belief in one's abilities, skills, and judgment, while self-efficacy is the belief in one's capacity to accomplish specific tasks and achieve goals.

Confidence and self-efficacy play crucial roles in goal setting and pursuit. Those with solid confidence are more inclined to tackle challenges, persist through setbacks, and ultimately succeed. Belief in one's capabilities enhances motivation and dedication, fostering more remarkable achievement.

Confidence and self-efficacy serve as shields against adversity. Individuals with high confidence exhibit resilience and are better prepared to rebound from setbacks. They perceive obstacles as opportunities for personal growth rather than impassable hurdles, enabling them to persevere in adverse circumstances. Through nurturing these attributes, individuals can navigate life's trials with increased resilience and accomplish their aspirations with unwavering confidence and resolve.

Building confidence and self-efficacy fosters personal growth and development. As individuals challenge themselves and succeed in various endeavors, their confidence grows, leading to increased self-esteem and a sense of accomplishment. This positive cycle of achievement and confidence fuels further growth and success. Confidence and self-efficacy enhance interpersonal skills and communication abilities. Individuals confident in themselves are more assertive, persuasive, and effective communicators. They can express their needs, advocate for themselves, and establish positive relationships with others.

Research has consistently shown the significant impact of confidence and self-efficacy on mental health. The study by Jeronimus, B. F., Kotov, R., Riese, H., & Ormel, J. (2016) highlights the importance of considering self-efficacy beliefs in understanding mental health outcomes. Muris, P. (2002) examines the relationship between self-efficacy beliefs and symptoms of anxiety disorders and depression in adolescents, shedding light on the protective role of self-efficacy in mental health. People with high confidence levels are less likely to experience stress, anxiety, and depression. Believing in one's abilities promotes a sense of empowerment and control over one's life, leading to greater overall happiness and fulfillment.

Building Confidence and Self-efficacy Exercise

List three achievements or successes you have experienced in the past.

1	
2	
3	

What are the skills, strengths, or qualities contributed to these successes?

How can you apply these same skills or qualities to overcome current challenges or setbacks you are or may be facing?

Practicing Self-compassion

Self-compassion involves treating oneself with kindness and acceptance during challenging moments. It involves three main components: self-kindness, recognizing common humanity, and mindfulness. Self-kindness means being gentle and patient with oneself rather than self-critical. Common humanity involves acknowledging that challenges are part of the human experience, fostering a sense of connection with others. Mindfulness entails approaching one's experiences with nonjudgmental awareness.

Practicing self-compassion is essential for maintaining emotional well-being and fostering resilience in facing life's challenges. Individuals can respond to difficult emotions with kindness and understanding through self-compassion rather than self-criticism or judgment. Acknowledging their struggles with compassion allows individuals to navigate adversity with greater emotional resilience and stability.

Self-compassion has been associated with reduced stress and anxiety levels. When people respond to their difficulties with kindness and acceptance, they are less inclined to dwell on negative thoughts or engage in self-criticism, factors that can heighten stress and anxiety.

A meta-analysis aggregates results from numerous studies examining the correlation between self-compassion and overall well-being. The analysis concludes that self-compassion demonstrates a positive connection with various facets of psychological wellness, such as life contentment and positive emotions (Zessin et al.; S., 2015).

Self-compassion promotes a healthier sense of self-worth and self-esteem. Instead of basing their self-worth on external achievements or comparisons to others, individuals who practice self-compassion learn to value themselves intrinsically, leading to a more stable and authentic self-esteem.

When individuals experience setbacks or failures, self-compassion allows them to respond with self-acceptance and understanding rather than harsh self-criticism. This compassionate approach to failure fosters resilience and encourages individuals to persevere in facing challenges.

Practicing self-compassion is a crucial aspect of emotional well-being and resilience. When individuals treat themselves with kindness, acceptance, and understanding, they can develop a more positive relationship with themselves. The positive relationship helps individuals better cope with life's challenges.

Practicing Self-compassion Exercise

Think about a recent setback or failure that left you feeling disappointed or discouraged:

| |
| |

Write three compassionate and encouraging statements you can say to yourself in response to this setback:

1
2
3

Reflect on how you treat yourself with kindness and understanding during challenging times.

I acknowledge:

Setbacks are a natural part of the learning and growth process.

Write what you would say to a loved family member or a dear friend if they are experiencing a setback or failure:

Read the above to yourself three times.

Enhancing Emotional Intelligence

Emotional intelligence, as defined by Mayer et al. (2008), pertains to the capacity to identify, comprehend, and proficiently control one's own emotions as well as the emotions of others. This construct encompasses a range of skills, such as self-awareness, self-regulation, empathy, and social aptitude.

Individuals with high emotional intelligence show a keen awareness of their emotions and can regulate them constructively, allowing them to cope with stress more effectively (Salovey & Mayer, 1990). They can empathize with others' feelings and perspectives, facilitating more meaningful and authentic interpersonal connections (Goleman, 1995).

Enhancing emotional intelligence is essential for navigating interpersonal relationships, enabling individuals to communicate more effectively, resolve conflicts amicably, and build stronger rapport with others (Brackett & Salovey, 2006). Emotional intelligence significantly influences leadership effectiveness, enabling leaders with high emotional intelligence to inspire and motivate their teams, promote collaboration, and navigate organizational complexities more effectively (Goleman, 2000).

Studies indicate that individuals with elevated emotional intelligence demonstrate greater resilience and adaptability when facing challenges. They excel in regulating emotions and sustaining a positive mindset, particularly during adverse circumstances (Mayer & Salovey, 1997). Cultivating emotional intelligence contributes to overall well-being and life satisfaction, enabling individuals to navigate life's trials with greater ease and equanimity (Brackett et al., 2011).

Enhancing emotional intelligence is crucial for achieving personal and professional success, fostering stronger interpersonal relationships, managing stress effectively, and promoting overall well-being and fulfillment.

Enhancing Emotional Intelligence Exercise

List three emotions you often experience. How aware are you of these emotions now?

Recognize the triggers for these emotions:

Reflect on recent interactions. How did you react emotionally? How did you respond? Are there other alternative ways you could have handled the situation more effectively?

Reflect on recent interactions. How well did you understand others' perspectives and emotions without judgment?

Identify a social situation where you can practice effective communication and interpersonal skills.

Set goal for the interaction (building rapport, resolving conflict):

Reflect afterward and identify areas for improvement.

Reflect on the entire exercise and identify specific actions you can take to continue developing your emotional intelligence skills.

Cultivating a triumphant mindset is an ongoing process that requires practice and commitment. Our journey through exploring personal triumphs has been rich with insights and transformative strategies. We have learned to celebrate achievements, embrace setbacks as growth opportunities, and cultivate a triumph mindset. We have discovered resilience by honoring our successes, reframing failures, and adopting positive outlooks. Apply these strategies, celebrate triumphs, and embrace challenges with confidence. You will continue to grow, thrive, and triumph over adversity through this.

Navigating turbulent times requires a multifaceted approach encompassing emotional resilience, adaptive coping strategies, and cultivating a supportive network. By implementing the strategies outlined in this guide, individuals can bolster their resilience, maintain their well-being, and emerge stronger from life's challenges. From fostering a growth mindset to practicing self-compassion, setting boundaries, and seeking positive outlets for stress relief, each strategy plays a crucial role in fostering inner strength and fortitude. As we journey through life's challenges, let us remember that resilience is not about avoiding difficulties but embracing them as opportunities for growth and transformation. With perseverance, self-awareness, and a resilient mindset, we can navigate even the most turbulent waters with courage and grace.

CHAPTER 6

Mapping Your Course: Goal Setting and Planning

"The secret of getting ahead is getting started. The secret of getting started is breaking your complex overwhelming tasks into small manageable tasks, and then starting on the first one."

—---- Mark Twain

This chapter is a call to action—a directive to chart your course with meaningful goals aligned with your purpose. Through meticulous planning, you create a navigational blueprint, guiding you through the currents of change. Imagine each goal as a landmark, contributing to the evolving map of your life's journey.

Goal Setting and Planning involve defining realistic and meaningful goals that align with your overarching purpose. It encompasses creating a step-by-step plan that outlines the actions, milestones, and resources required to achieve these goals.

Goal setting provides a sense of purpose and direction. It helps individuals define their goals and sets the course for their actions. Goals function as a source of motivation. They give individuals a reason to strive for improvement and focus on their aspirations. Goals provide measurable criteria for success. Goal setting allows individuals to track their progress, celebrate achievements, and identify areas for improvement. Goal setting helps make informed decisions. Individuals with a clear vision of their objectives can assess choices based on their alignment with those goals.

Planning involves allocating time effectively. It helps individuals prioritize tasks, manage deadlines, and allocate resources efficiently.

Goal-oriented planning streamlines efforts. It enables individuals to concentrate on tasks that contribute directly to their objectives, reducing distractions and unnecessary activities. Setting and achieving goals fosters personal and professional growth. It pushes individuals beyond their comfort zones, encouraging the development of new skills and capabilities. Reaching goals boosts self-esteem and confidence. It reinforces the belief that individuals can overcome challenges and achieve desired outcomes. Planning involves considering potential obstacles and developing strategies to overcome them. Individuals are better equipped to face challenges with effective goal setting, fostering a proactive and responsible mindset by taking ownership of their actions and progress. Goals help individuals align their actions with their values. This alignment facilitates decision-making that is consistent with personal principles and long-term objectives. Goals give individuals a sense of purpose and direction, contributing to overall well-being. It provides a framework for a meaningful and fulfilling life.

Planning involves identifying and utilizing resources efficiently. It includes financial, time, and human resources, ensuring optimal use to achieve desired outcomes. While planning, individuals consider various scenarios and potential changes. This flexibility enhances adaptability, allowing individuals to adjust their course in response to unforeseen circumstances.

In short, goal setting and planning provide direction, motivation, and a structured approach to personal and professional pursuits. They contribute to growth, well-being, and realizing one's full potential.

This strategic approach empowers individuals to navigate their life's journey with purposeful direction and measurable progress. Use the following worksheets to articulate your goals, align them with your purpose, and develop a structured plan for achievement.

Crafting Your Goal Map

What overarching purpose or vision guides your life? Consider your values, passions, and long-term aspirations (refer to the Values Clarification Exercise in Chapter 2).

```



```

List three specific and realistic goals that align with your purpose.

1
2
3

How do each of the identified goals contribute to or align with your overarching purpose?

1
2
3

Break down each goal into smaller components or milestones. What steps are necessary to achieve these goals?

How will you measure the success of each goal? Identify specific metrics or indicators that signal progress.

1	
2	
3	

Set realistic timelines for each goal and its milestones. Consider short-term and long-term deadlines.

	Short Term Deadline	Long Term Goals Deadline
1		
2		
3		

Outline specific actions you need to take to progress towards each milestone.

What resources, whether financial, educational, or social, are needed to achieve your goals?

What are potential obstacles or challenges that may arise?

What are some of the strategies you have for overcoming or navigating these challenges?

Write a personal commitment statement for each goal. Affirm your dedication to working towards these objectives.

1	
2	
3	

What practical steps can you initiate today?

How often will you assess your goals, and what adjustments might be necessary?

Identify ways to celebrate each milestone:

Use this worksheet as a dynamic tool for clarifying your goals, aligning them with your purpose, and creating a roadmap for achievement. Regularly revisit and adjust your plan as needed, ensuring it remains a guiding force on your journey.

Goal Setting Worksheet

Values and Passions That Matter to Me

Identify areas of your life or aspects of your work that align with your values and priorities.

Visualize Your Ideal Future:

Envision where you want to be in the long term—both personally and professionally.

Consider aspects such as career, relationships, health, personal growth, and overall well-being.

Break down long-term goals into short-term goals (specific and achievable with a timeframe, contributing to your long-term vision).

Use the SMART goal setting Criteria.

Specific: Clearly define the goal with specific details. Be precise about what you want to achieve.

Example: Instead of a vague goal like "exercise more," make it specific, such as "run for 30 minutes three times a week."

Measurable: Establish criteria to measure progress and determine when the goal is achieved.

Example: Instead of saying "lose weight," make it measurable, like "lose 10 pounds in two months."

Achievable: Ensure that the goal is realistic and attainable. Consider your resources and capabilities.

Example: If your goal is to learn a new language, make sure it's achievable given your available time and resources.

Relevant: Ensure that the goal aligns with your broader objectives and is relevant to your overall vision.

Example: If your long-term goal is career advancement, a relevant goal might be "complete a certification course."

Time-bound: Set a specific timeframe for achieving the goal. This adds a sense of urgency and helps in monitoring progress.

Example: Instead of saying "write a book," make it time-bound, like "complete the first draft of the book within six months."

Example: Instead of saying "losing weight by running", complete it by stating "Run for 30 minutes, three times a week, to lose 10 lbs. in two months".

Prioritize your goals based on their importance and urgency. Identify which goals will have the most significant impact on your life or work.

Break each goal down into actionable steps. Outline specific actions you need to take to achieve each goal.

Assign realistic deadlines to each goal and its corresponding action steps.

Affirmations

I will regularly review my progress toward each goal.

I will adjust my action plans and timelines if needed.

I will celebrate my achievements.

I will reevaluate my long-term vision periodically and adjust my

goals accordingly.

I can share my goals with supportive friends, family, or colleagues.

I can find an accountability partner to help me stay on track.

I understand the goal-setting process as a continuous learning

experience.

I may refine my approach based on what works best for me.

Following these goal-setting instructions can create a roadmap for personal and professional success, providing direction and purpose in navigating change with intention.

SMART Goal Setting

SMART goal setting uses the SMART criteria (Specific, Measurable, Achievable, Relevant, Time-bound) to set clear and actionable goals. Specific goals are clear and well-defined, with a specific outcome in mind. Measurable goals have criteria for tracking progress and determining success. Achievable goals are realistic and within reach, given available resources and constraints. Relevant goals align with broader objectives and contribute to overall success. Time-bound goals have a defined timeline or deadline for completion, providing a sense of urgency and accountability. This approach helps individuals set clear, achievable, and impactful goals that drive meaningful progress.

Example of a SMART Goal:

Specific: Lose 10 pounds by the end of the year.

Measurable: Track weight loss progress weekly using a scale and journal.

Achievable: Commit to exercising for at least 30 minutes five days a week and reducing daily calorie intake by 500 calories.

Relevant: Improving health and increasing energy levels are important personal priorities.

Time-bound: Achieve the goal within six months, with regular check-ins every two weeks to monitor progress and adjust as needed.

My SMART Goal Setting

Identify the area of your life you want to focus on (e.g., career, health, relationships, finances, personal growth).

Specific: What exactly do you want to accomplish? Be clear and precise.

Measurable: How will you know when you have achieved your goal? Include measurable indicators.

Achievable: Is your goal realistic and attainable given your resources and circumstances?

Relevant: Does your goal align with your values, priorities, and long-term objectives?

Time-bound: When do you aim to achieve your goal? Set a deadline for completion.

In one sentence, describe your goal with SMART criteria:

Goal Prioritization Techniques

Goal prioritization is a fundamental aspect of effective time management and productivity, essential for success in various aspects of life. Individuals can optimize their efforts and resources toward achieving their most significant objectives by systematically organizing and ranking their goals based on their importance and urgency (Jones & Briscoe, 2016). This prioritization process provides clarity and focus, allowing individuals to direct their energy towards tasks that align with their overarching aspirations and values.

Enhancing the prioritization of goals can enhance decision-making, enabling individuals to evaluate choices by their alignment with more important goals (Covey, 1989). This ensures that time and resources are allocated wisely, and efforts are directed towards activities that generate the greatest impact. By prioritizing goals, individuals can enhance their time management skills, allocate their time efficiently, and meet deadlines without feeling overwhelmed (McKeown, 2014).

Prioritizing goals reduces stress and increases motivation by breaking tasks into manageable steps. (Allen, 2001). By focusing on one goal at a time, individuals can avoid feeling overwhelmed and maintain momentum toward achieving their objectives. This sense of progress and accomplishment boosts motivation and encourages continued effort toward success (Duhigg, 2012).

Goal prioritization promotes alignment with personal values and long-term objectives, ensuring that individuals pursue goals that align with their aspirations (Sinek, 2009). This alignment fosters a sense of purpose and fulfillment as individuals work toward objectives that resonate with their values and vision for the future.

The Eisenhower Matrix, also known as the Urgent/Important Matrix, is a productivity and time management tool developed by former U.S. President Dwight D. Eisenhower. While there is no specific source where Eisenhower formally introduced the matrix, its principles align with his reputed approach to productivity and decision-making. The matrix has been widely popularized and adapted in various productivity books, articles, and resources on time management. The matrix categorizes tasks into four quadrants:

Important and Urgent: Tasks require urgent focus and directly contributing to goal attainment or addressing pressing matters. These tasks are top priority and should be dealt with promptly.

Important but Not Urgent: Tasks that are significant for long-term goals and personal growth do not require immediate action. It is vital to schedule tasks before they become urgent.

Urgent but Not Important: Tasks that demand urgent action yet offer minimal contribution to overarching objectives or essential priorities. These tasks often involve interruptions or distractions and should be minimized or delegated whenever possible.

Not Important and Not Urgent: Tasks categorized as neither urgent nor important may be deemed as time-wasting activities or distractions. To concentrate on more important tasks, it is advisable to either eliminate or reduce these activities.

The Eisenhower Matrix

Important and Urgent	Urgent but Not Important
Important but Not Urgent	**Not Important and Not Urgent**

You can also use the ABCD method to categorize and prioritize your goals. It is similar to the Eisenhower Matrix but lists the tasks in order of priority in a more visual manner.

The ABCD Method

A: Important and Urgent

B: Important but Not Urgent

C: Urgent but Not Important

D: Not Important and Not Urgent

Feel free to experiment with both methods to find the one that works for you.

Goal Visualization

Goal visualization is a powerful technique to clarify objectives by creating vivid mental images of desired achievements (Naylor & Briggs, 1989). This technique helps individuals articulate their aspirations and develop concrete plans to achieve them (Bandler & Grinder, 1979). By visualizing their goals, people can mentally picture themselves achieving them, which boosts motivation and inspires them to take actionable steps (Krosnick & Alwin, 1987). Visualization helps individuals focus on goals and desired outcomes (Clark, 2010). Consistently visualizing these goals helps people concentrate on them, prioritize tasks, and stay committed to achieving their objectives (Loehr & Schwartz, 2003). Visualizing successful goal attainment enhances confidence and self-assurance (Lane, 2012). By visualizing overcoming obstacles, individuals strengthen their belief in their ability to succeed, increasing resilience and perseverance (Bandura, 1997).

Visualization engages the subconscious mind and profoundly influences thoughts, emotions, and behaviors (Langer, 1989). Through repeated visualization, individuals can program their subconscious to align their actions and behaviors with goal attainment, increasing their chances of success (LeDoux, 2012). Visualization also serves as a powerful tool for reducing anxiety and stress associated with pursuing goals (Gross & Levenson, 1997). By mentally practicing successful outcomes, one can feel prepared and confident, diminishing uncertainty (Hornsey et al., 2015).

In conclusion, goal visualization offers a comprehensive approach to achieving goals, empowering individuals to clarify their objectives, boosting motivation, maintaining focus, enhancing confidence, aligning behaviors, and alleviating stress throughout their pursuit of success.

Goal Visualization Exercise

Specify 3 realistic and attainable goals:

1	
2	
3	

Close your eyes and imagine yourself achieving your goals. What would that look like? Write it after you complete your images. Be specific.

Visualize the details of success, including how it feels, looks, and sounds.

Reflect on the emotions and sensations that arise during this visualization.

Action Planning

Action planning is a structured process that involves defining specific steps or tasks to achieve a desired goal or objective. It entails breaking down bigger goals into more manageable actions, creating timelines, allocating resources, and assigning responsibilities to individuals or teams. The main aim of action planning is to provide a roadmap for implementation, guiding the systematic execution of tasks. This involves establishing specific goals, recognizing possible obstacles or difficulties, and crafting plans to address them effectively. The ultimate purpose of action planning is to transform goals into actionable steps, ensuring progress toward desired outcomes and enabling effective decision-making.

Action Planning Exercise

Create a step-by-step action plan for each goal. Break down tasks into smaller action steps and schedule them into your calendar. Regularly review and adjust your plan as needed to stay on track.

What is the specific goal you want to achieve (Make sure it is SMART, Specific, Measurable, Achievable, Relevant, Time-bound).

Break down your goal into smaller tasks or actions that will contribute to its achievement.

Task 1	Actions/Steps
Task 2	Actions/Steps
Task 3	Actions/Steps
Task 4	Actions/Steps
Task 5	Actions/Steps

Organize your tasks in order of priority. Identify which tasks are essential to accomplish first and which can wait.

1) For each task, break it down into even smaller action steps. These should be specific, actionable tasks that can be completed in a reasonable amount of time.

2) Identifying resources: Identify resources you may need to complete each task, such as time, money, materials, or assistance from others.

3) Monitor Progress: Regularly review your action plan to track your progress. Update your plan as needed, adjusting deadlines or tasks as circumstances change.

4) Journaling: Keep a reflective journal to track progress, reflect on notable

experiences, and identify areas for improvement. Write about your successes, setbacks, and lessons learned along the way. Regular reflection can help you stay focused, motivated, and resilient in pursuing your goals.

5) Sharing: It's important to share your goals with people you trust, like a friend, mentor, or coach. Set up regular check-ins to review your progress, discuss any challenges, and celebrate your accomplishments. Having someone to hold you accountable makes it more likely for you to stay motivated and committed to achieving your goals.

6) Celebrate accomplishments: Reward yourself for completing tasks. Remain flexible as you work toward your goals. Be open to adjusting your action plan as necessary to overcome challenges or seize opportunities.

Action Planning Worksheet

Tasks	Deadline	Resources Needed
a: _____ Action steps _____ _____ _____	_____ _____ _____ _____	
b: _____ Action steps _____ _____ _____	_____ _____ _____ _____	
c: _____ Action steps _____ _____ _____	_____ _____ _____ _____	
d: _____ Action steps _____ _____ _____	_____ _____ _____	
e: _____ Action steps _____ _____ _____	_____ _____ _____ _____	

Goal Evaluation

Goal evaluation is a crucial component of personal and professional development that offers various advantages. It allows individuals to gauge their progress, fostering a sense of accountability and concentration. It facilitates learning by providing valuable insights into practical strategies and areas needing improvement. Goal evaluation also enhances motivation and satisfaction by recognizing achievements and pinpointing areas that require further enhancement. It promotes adaptability and resilience by encouraging flexibility in response to challenges. In short, goal evaluation is indispensable for continuous improvement and achieving success.

It is crucial to ensure that your goals align with your purpose by connecting them to your core values, passions, and long-term objectives. When your goals align with your purpose, they become more meaningful, motivating, and fulfilling. This alignment helps you remain focused, driven, and resilient when facing challenges. It enables you to prioritize tasks and make decisions that align with your overarching purpose, resulting in greater satisfaction and accomplishment. Ultimately, aligning your goals with your purpose allows you to create an authentic, purposeful life that is true to who you are (Locke, 2002).

In the following evaluation exercise, reflect on your top 5 core values and enter them in order of importance in the chart below. Write your current short-term and long-term goals. Evaluate each goal to see if it is in alignment with your values. Put YES in the coordinating box if the goal aligns with your value(s); put NO if the goal does not align with your value(s).

Goal -Value Alignment Evaluation

Values Goals	Value #1	Value #2	Value #3	Value #4	Value #5
Goal #1					
Goal #2					
Goal #3					
Goal #4					
Goal #5					

Are there any goals that are not in harmony with your core values? If so, how are you going to redefine your goal to align it with your fundamental values?

Goal Evaluation Exercise

Goal Description
Current Progress
Successes
Challenges
Lessons Learned
Adjustments
Next Steps
Timeline

Goal setting is more than outlining objectives; it aligns the objectives with our deepest values and long-term aspirations. By engaging in reflective exercises, SMART goal setting, and strategic planning, we lay the foundation for a purpose-driven journey toward personal and professional fulfillment. Evaluating our current goals helps us stay on track and aligned with our values and vision. As we embark on this journey of goal setting and planning, let us remain steadfast in our commitment to aligning our actions with our purpose, knowing that each step brings us closer to realizing our dreams and living a life of significance.

CHAPTER 7

The Power of Adaptation: Flexibility and Flow

"It is not the strongest of the species that survive, nor the most intelligent, but the one most responsive to change."" —---- *Charles Darwin*

In the ever-changing landscape of life, the ability to adapt is paramount. This chapter explores the significance of adaptability and the transformative power of cultivating a flexible mindset. Through case studies and practical insights, we embrace change and navigate life's twists and turns with resilience and grace.

Flexibility and flow refer to recognizing and embracing change and cultivating a mindset that thrives in dynamic environments. It involves understanding the importance of adaptability in navigating life's challenges and opportunities. Developing a flexible mindset entail embracing change as a constant and fostering continuous personal and professional growth through resilience, learning, and openness to new experiences.

Adaptability is a crucial aspect of both success and well-being in the face of life's ever-changing circumstances. Recognizing that change is inevitable in personal relationships, careers, and society, adaptable individuals can navigate transitions with resilience and composure (Ryff & Singer, 2003). In today's dynamic professional world, adaptability is essential for staying relevant, thriving in careers, and seizing new opportunities (Griffin & Hesketh, 2003). It also plays a role in resilience, helping individuals bounce back from adversity, learn valuable lessons, and become stronger (Tugade & Fredrickson, 2004). Adaptable individuals embrace new ideas and perspectives, fostering creativity and innovation in problem-solving (Ashford et al., 2003). Socially, adaptability is crucial for adjusting communication styles, empathizing with others, and building positive relationships (Martin & Rubin, 1995). It also contributes to emotional resilience, aiding individuals in coping with stress and uncertainties, promoting continuous learning and effective leadership (Wong & Wong, 2006).

By embracing change as an opportunity for personal growth, adaptability catalyzes ongoing development, facilitating continuous growth and realizing untapped potential (Martin-Krumm & Tarquinio, 2019). Ultimately, it empowers individuals to survive and thrive, encouraging them to embrace possibilities and navigate life's complexities with resilience and optimism (Carver, 1998).

Cultivating a Flexible Mindset

A flexible mindset involves adaptability and openness to change, enabling individuals to adjust attitudes and behaviors in response to challenges. It fosters resilience in the face of uncertainty, viewing setbacks as opportunities for growth. This mindset facilitates creativity, innovation, and problem-solving skills, allowing individuals to navigate diverse environments with agility and resilience.

Take, for instance, an individual facing unexpected job loss due to company restructuring. Rather than succumbing to feelings of overwhelm, they adopt a flexible mindset. They see the job loss as a chance to explore alternative career avenues or acquire skills in a different field. By maintaining adaptability and receptivity, they eventually discover a rewarding career opportunity they had not envisioned.

Studies indicate that individuals with a flexible mindset demonstrate enhanced abilities to manage stress and overcome challenges, fostering resilience, well-being, and achievement (Fergus & Zimmerman, 2005). Cultivating flexibility has been linked to improved problem-solving skills, creativity, and adaptability (Bergomi et al., 2013). A flexible mindset enhances interpersonal relationships by fostering empathy, understanding, and cooperation. Being receptive to different viewpoints and approaches can improve communication and strengthen connections.

Cultivating a flexible mindset is paramount for thriving in today's dynamic world. By embracing change, learning from experiences, and remaining adaptable, individuals can navigate life's challenges with resilience, confidence, and success.

Complete the following exercises to explore and cultivate a flexible mindset for adaptation. Reflect on each prompt and consider how you can integrate adaptability into your daily life. Use this worksheet as a tool for cultivating a flexible and adaptable mindset. Embrace change. See it as a chance for growth. Every challenge can enhance your adaptability.

Cultivating a Flexible Mindset

List three significant changes you have experienced recently, whether personal or professional.

1	
2	
3	

What are your initial reactions to these changes? Were they positive, negative, or a mix of emotions?

Can you recall three ways being adaptable has benefited you in the past? How did adaptability contribute to positive outcomes?

1	
2	
3	

Think of a situation where you held a strong belief. How flexible were you in reconsidering or adapting your perspective when faced with new information?

List two skills or subjects you've never explored but would be willing to learn. How can embracing these new areas contribute to your personal growth?

1	
2	

Recall the last time you tried something new. How did it make you feel, and what did you learn from the experience?

Consider a situation where the outcome was uncertain. How did you navigate the uncertainty, and what did you learn from the experience?

Anticipate a potential change in your life. Develop a plan on how you can approach this change with adaptability and a flexible mindset.

Recall a time when your adaptability led to a positive outcome. Celebrate and acknowledge your ability to adapt.

To showcase the transformative potential of adaptability, we explore real-life scenarios where people overcome challenges with grace and resilience. These stories emphasize the significance of being flexible and resilient to overcome obstacles and succeed. They cover a range of experiences, including career changes and personal challenges. Through these inspiring examples, we gain valuable insights into the art of adaptation and the limitless potential of the human spirit. These stories serve as beacons of hope, providing real-life examples of resilience, courage, and personal triumph. The purpose is to draw lessons and motivation from these narratives, offering insights that inspire readers to view change as a gateway to personal evolution and growth.

Oprah Winfrey, renowned as one of the most influential media personalities globally, has traversed a journey marked by formidable challenges. Born into poverty in rural Mississippi and enduring a tumultuous childhood marred by abuse and instability, Oprah faced adversity from a tender age. However, rather than succumbing to her circumstances, she exhibited remarkable resilience and determination to transcend her upbringing.

Against all odds, Oprah found solace and refuge in education and performance, excelling academically, and showing innate talent as a speaker and presenter. Her innate charisma and unwavering drive propelled her into the realm of media, where she embarked on a career that would eventually redefine the television landscape.

Beyond her extraordinary success in the entertainment industry, Oprah has leveraged her platform for philanthropic endeavors, championing causes related to education, healthcare, and social justice. Through initiatives like the Oprah Winfrey Foundation and the Oprah Winfrey Leadership Academy for Girls, she has empowered countless individuals, particularly women and children, to overcome adversity and pursue their dreams. Oprah's life story is a testament to the power of resilience, determination, and self-belief in overcoming adversity and achieving extraordinary success.

Sophia's journey began with a heartbreaking loss that shattered her world when she lost her parents in a tragic car accident. At the tender age of 23, she found herself thrust into the role of caretaker for her teenage brother, grappling with grief, shock, and overwhelming responsibility. Despite the weight of her circumstances, Sophia refused to let despair consume her. Drawing strength from her support network and seeking solace in therapy, Sophia embarked on a journey of healing and resilience. With each passing day, she slowly navigated the complexities of her new reality, embracing her role as a "single parent" to her brother with unwavering determination and love.

Amidst the emotional turmoil, Sophia faced the practical challenges of balancing caregiving responsibilities with the demands of her career. Fueled by resilience and a relentless drive to provide for her brother, she courageously pursued career changes and opportunities to secure their financial stability. As time passed, Sophia's resilience and unwavering commitment bore fruit.

Despite her hardships, she found purpose and fulfillment as a caregiver and provider. Her journey of loss and rebuilding transformed her into a beacon of strength and inspiration, demonstrating the remarkable capacity of the human spirit to endure, adapt, and thrive in the face of adversity.

Amelia's life took an unexpected turn when, at 42, she was hit with a double blow: losing her job and facing the dissolution of her marriage, leaving her to care for her aging parents and two teenage children. Faced with these devastating setbacks, Amelia could have easily succumbed to despair and resignation. However, she chose a different path—a path of resilience, courage, and reinvention.

Rather than allowing herself to be defined by her circumstances, Amelia saw this as an opportunity for personal growth and transformation. Drawing strength from within, she refused to let adversity dictate her future. With unwavering determination and a resilient spirit, Amelia embarked on a journey of self-discovery and renewal.

Amelia began by prioritizing self-care, recognizing the importance of nurturing her physical, emotional, and mental well-being during this challenging time. She found solace and strength amidst the chaos through meditation, exercise, and journaling.

As Amelia delved deeper into her journey of self-exploration, she unearthed a passion for helping others navigate similar challenges. Leveraging her years of experience and expertise in public speaking, she started her own life coaching business, offering guidance and support to individuals facing career transitions, relationship difficulties, and personal setbacks.

Amelia's coaching business gained momentum with new clients inspired by her resilience and wisdom despite her initial uncertainties and doubts. Through her compassionate guidance and unwavering positivity, she became a beacon of hope for those struggling to overcome adversity.

As her business flourished, Amelia found herself rebuilding her life and discovering a newfound sense of purpose and fulfillment. She transformed her life by embracing change and turning her pain into a catalyst for growth. She became a source of inspiration and empowerment for countless others facing similar challenges. Amelia's story is a powerful reminder of the resilience of the human spirit and the boundless possibilities that arise when we dare to embrace adversity as an opportunity for growth and renewal.

Melody's life took a significant turn when her youngest daughter left for college, leaving her with an empty nest and a profound sense of loss. As a full-time mom of three children, Melody had dedicated herself to nurturing and caring for her family, finding fulfillment and purpose in her role as a mother. However, with her children now departing on their journeys, Melody grappled with feelings of sadness, loneliness, and uncertainty about her identity and purpose in life.

Amidst the emotional turbulence, Melody recognized the need for a fresh perspective and a flexible mindset to navigate this new chapter of her life. Seeking guidance and support, she embarked on a journey of self-discovery through therapy sessions, delving into her innermost thoughts and emotions to gain clarity and insight into her desires and aspirations.

Upon introspection, Melody rediscovered her passion for teaching that had been overshadowed by motherhood. Fueled by a newfound sense of purpose and determination, she took proactive steps to pursue her dream, enrolling in courses to obtain the credentials to become a teacher.

Despite the challenges and uncertainties ahead, Melody approached her journey with resilience, adaptability, and an unwavering commitment to personal growth and fulfillment. With each hurdle she faced, she embraced the opportunity for growth and transformation, viewing setbacks as steppingstones rather than roadblocks.

As Melody immersed herself in her studies and preparation for her new career, she experienced profound empowerment and liberation. Rediscovering her passion for teaching reignited her sense of purpose and provided a renewed sense of identity and fulfillment. With her flexible mindset and unwavering determination, Melody embarked on a new chapter of her life with optimism, resilience, and a deep sense of fulfillment.

Reflect on the case studies in the previous paragraphs and write about how they relate to your own experiences and journey. Please respond to the following questions to enhance your comprehension and relationship with the material.

Connecting Others' Stories to Your Journey

Write down the main themes or messages conveyed through the stories.

Reflect on which themes resonate most strongly with you and why.

Are there moments in your life that parallel those described in the stories?

What emotions and memories did the stories stir up?

What aspects of the story motivate and inspire you?

What lessons or insights can you draw from the stories? How do these lessons apply to your own life?

Reflecting on others' narratives can be a powerful tool for self-discovery and growth. Connecting these stories with your own experiences will better understand yourself and the world around you. Use this worksheet as a guide to explore the insights gained from the stories shared in the text and apply them to your journey.

The power of adaptation lies within each of us. By recognizing the importance of adaptability, developing a flexible mindset, and drawing inspiration from real-life examples of successful adaptation, we can navigate life's challenges with confidence and resilience. As we embrace change and flow with the currents of life, we unlock new opportunities for growth, fulfillment, and personal transformation.

CHAPTER 8

Your Personal Workbook: Applying Insights to Your Life

"Knowledge without action is meaningless." —-- *Abu Bakr*

As this transformative journey reaches its zenith, the focus shifts to active application. Engage in interactive exercises that prompt you to apply the insights gained throughout this odyssey. Picture creating a personalized workbook—a tangible manifestation of your journey, a testament to your commitment to navigate life's currents with purpose, resilience, and the triumph of intentional living.

Your Personal Workbook is a dynamic tool designed to facilitate a hands-on application of the insights and concepts gained throughout your transformative journey. It serves as a bridge between theoretical understanding and practical implementation, providing a structured space for interactive exercises tailored to your unique experiences. This workbook is a dedicated platform for ongoing reflection, growth, and intentional navigation through life's transformative currents.

Reflective Insights

Implementing insights into your life is essential for personal growth and development. While acquiring knowledge and grasping new concepts are valuable endeavors, genuine transformation occurs when you apply these insights practically. Integrating insights into your daily life can convert theoretical understanding into concrete actions and behaviors. This active engagement allows you to test hypotheses, experiment with alternative approaches, and adjust strategies based on real-world experiences. It empowers you to confront challenges, surmount obstacles, and make substantial progress toward your objectives.

Applying insights also nurtures self-awareness by prompting reflection on your values, priorities, and aspirations. Through this introspective process, you gain a deeper understanding of yourself and your motivations, enhancing personal growth and fulfillment. By incorporating insights into your everyday routines, you can cultivate positive habits, attain greater satisfaction, and lead a more purpose-driven and meaningful life.

Summarize the key insights gained from the book. What concepts resonated with you the most?

Recognize specific challenges or areas in your life where you feel the need for change and growth.

Evaluate your current lifestyle against your core values. Identify areas where alignment is strong and where adjustments are needed.

Personal Growth Strategies

Develop a plan for enhancing your adaptability. List strategies to embrace change and cultivate a flexible mindset.

Outline actions to cultivate resilience. How will you navigate challenges with strength and perseverance?

Envisioning Your Future

Envision your future self. What aspects of your life do you see transformed, and what steps will lead you there?

Applying Concepts

Based on the book's teachings, set realistic and meaningful short-term and long-term goals aligned with your values.

Create a visual or written tracker to monitor your progress toward set goals. Celebrate successes and learn from setbacks.

Write a personal purpose statement that reflects your aspirations and values.

Joyful Practices

List activities that bring you joy and contribute to emotional well-being. Schedule regular moments for these practices.

Develop a self-care plan with specific activities that contribute to physical, mental, and emotional well-being.

Continuous Learning

Keep a log of insights and lessons learned from new experiences. How are you incorporating continuous learning into your life?

Regularly reflect on how you've adapted to recent changes. What growth opportunities emerged?

Inspirational Quotes

Collect quotes, images, and words that inspire you. Use them as daily reminders of your journey.

This workbook is a living document—constantly evolving and adapting alongside your journey. Regularly revisit and update it to ensure it remains a meaningful and effective tool for your personal development. As we conclude our journey through Navigating Life's Tides, reflecting on the profound exploration of change, growth, and purpose unfolding within these pages is important. This book has been more than a guide; it is a companion on your odyssey—a journey of self-discovery and transformation.

CONCLUSION

As we conclude this journey through Navigating Life's Tides: Embracing Change for Success, it's essential to reflect on the transformative insights gained and the pathways to personal growth we've explored together.

From the outset, we embarked on this journey with a clear purpose: to empower readers with the tools and perspectives needed to navigate life's ever-changing currents successfully. Drawing from personal experiences and professional insights, we delved into the profound wisdom of understanding change and embracing it as an opportunity for growth.

Through self-assessment and reflection, we've identified key areas in our lives where change is needed, laying the groundwork for meaningful transformation. With a growth mindset and a vision for a purpose-driven life, we've set sail towards a future aligned with our values and aspirations.

Navigating life's inevitable challenges and setbacks, we've cultivated resilience, discovered positive coping mechanisms, and drawn inspiration from real-life examples of triumph over adversity. Celebrating our personal triumphs along the way, we've cultivated gratitude and a deeper sense of fulfillment.

Mapping our course through goal setting and planning, we've set realistic and meaningful goals, creating step-by-step plans to achieve them and aligning them with our overarching purpose.

Recognizing the power of adaptation and flexibility, we've learned to embrace change with grace and resilience, drawing motivation from our own narratives and connecting them to the broader journey of personal growth.

As we conclude our exploration, we invite you to apply the insights gained to your own life through interactive exercises and the creation of a personalized workbook. May this journey serve as a catalyst for continued exploration, growth, and fulfillment as you navigate life's tides with courage and grace.

Upcoming books:

For upcoming books listed below, or suggestions for future publications, please email:

atrpublishing@gmail.com

Embracing Freedom: The Power of Letting Go
The Path to Inner Peace and Liberation

The Perspective Shift: Reimagining Your Life with Fresh Insight
Discovering Clarity, Purpose, and Joy Through Different Views

Love in Full Bloom: Cultivating Self-Compassion and Self-Love
Nurturing the Heart Within and Blossom into Wholeness

Togetherness: Creating Connection in a Disconnected World
Cultivating Meaningful Relationships and Shared Growth

The Path to True Happiness
Finding Fulfillment in Realistic Expectations

Forgiveness: The Path to Inner Freedom
Embrace Healing, Release Resentment, and Rediscover Joy

References

Algoe, S. B. (2012). Find, remind, and bind: The functions of gratitude in everyday relationships. Social and Personality Psychology Compass, 6(6), 455–469.

Allen, D. (2001). Getting things done: The art of stress-free productivity. Penguin.

Arnett, J. J. (2000). Emerging adulthood: A theory of development from the late teens through the twenties. American Psychologist, 55(5), 469-480.

Ashford, S. J., De Stobbeleir, K. E., & Nujella, M. (2003). To seek or not to seek: Is that the only question? Current directions in Psychological Science, 12(4), 209-213.

Bandler, R., & Grinder, J. (1979). Frogs into Princes: Neuro Linguistic Programming. Real People Press.

Bandura, A. (1997). Self-efficacy: The exercise of control. W. H. Freeman and Company.

Bergen-Cico, D., Possemato, K., & Cheon, S. (2018). Examining the feasibility and utility of utilizing mindful eating in residential weight management programs. Eating Behaviors, 30, 1-6.

Bergomi, C., Tschacher, W., & Kupper, Z. (2013). The assessment of mindfulness with self-report measures: Existing scales and open issues. Mindfulness, 4(3), 191-202.

Biddle, S. J., Fox, K. R., & Boutcher, S. H. (2000). Physical activity and psychological well-being. Routledge.

Bolier, L., Haverman, M., Westerhof, G. J., Riper, H., Smit, F., & Bohlmeijer, E. (2013). Positive psychology interventions: a meta-analysis of randomized controlled studies. BMC Public Health, 13(1), 119.

Bonanno, G. A. (2004). Loss, trauma, and human resilience: Have we underestimated the human capacity to thrive after extremely aversive events? American Psychologist, 59(1), 20–28.

Bonanno, G. A., Papa, A., Lalande, K., Westphal, M., & Coifman, K. (2004). The importance of being flexible: The ability to both enhance and suppress emotional expression predicts long-term adjustment. Psychological Science, 15(7), 482-487.

Brackett, M. A., Rivers, S. E., Shiffman, S., Lerner, N., & Salovey, P. (2011). Relating emotional abilities to social functioning: A comparison of self-report and performance measures of emotional intelligence. Journal of Personality and Social Psychology, 101(4), 881–898.

Brackett, M. A., & Salovey, P. (2006). Measuring emotional intelligence with the Mayer-Salovey-Caruso Emotional Intelligence Test (MSCEIT). In G. Geher (Ed.), Measuring emotional intelligence: Common ground and controversy (pp. 129-147). Nova Science Publishers.

Brown, K. W., & Ryan, R. M. (2003). The benefits of being present: Mindfulness and its role in psychological well-being. Journal of Personality and Social Psychology, 84(4), 822–848.

Buckingham, M., & Clifton, D. O. (2001). Now, Discover Your Strengths. Free Press.

Carstensen, L. L. (2006). The influence of a sense of time on human development. Science, 312(5782), 1913-1915.

Carver, C. S. (1998). Resilience and thriving: Issues, models, and linkages. Journal of Social Issues, 54(2), 245-266.

Carver, C. S., & Connor-Smith, J. (2010). Personality and coping. Annual Review of Psychology, 61, 679-704.

Carver, C. S., & Scheier, M. F. (2001). On the Self-Regulation of Behavior. Cambridge University Press.

Chiesa, A., Calati, R., & Serretti, A. (2011). Does mindfulness training improve cognitive abilities? A systematic review of neuropsychological findings. Clinical Psychology Review, 31(3), 449–464.

Clark, D. (2010). Visualizing success: A mental rehearsal primer. American Psychological Association.

Cloud, H., & Townsend, J. (1992). Boundaries: When to say yes, when to say no to take control of your life. Zondervan.

Cohen, S. (1985). Social support and health. Academic Press.

Covey, S. R. (1989). The 7 habits of highly effective people: Powerful lessons in personal change. Simon and Schuster.

Creating a Resilient Mindset with the Subconscious Mind . anthonymdavis.com. HTTPS://ANTHONYMDAVIS.COM/CREATING-A-RESILIENT-mindset-subconscious-mind/

de Saint-Exupéry, A. (1943). The Little Prince. Reynal & Hitchcock.

Deci, E. L., & Ryan, R. M. (1985). Intrinsic motivation and self-determination in human behavior. Plenum.

Duckworth, A. L., Peterson, C., Matthews, M. D., & Kelly, D. R. (2007). Grit: Perseverance and passion for long-term goals. Journal of Personality and Social Psychology, 92(6), 1087–1101.

Duckworth, A. L., & Quinn, P. D. (2009). Development and validation of the Short Grit Scale (GRIT–S). Journal of Personality Assessment, 91(2), 166–174.

Dweck, C. S. (2006). Mindset: The new psychology of success. Random House.

Ehrenreich, B. (2009). Bright-sided: How positive thinking is undermining America. Picador.

Emmons, R. A. (2007). Thanks!: How the new science of gratitude can make you happier. Houghton Mifflin Harcourt.

Emmons, R. A., & McCullough, M. E. (2003). Counting blessings versus burdens: An experimental investigation of gratitude and subjective well-being in daily life. Journal of Personality and Social Psychology, 84(2), 377–389.

Fixed Versus Growth Mindset - anxiety-stresscenter.com. HTTPS://ANXIETY-stresscenter.com/fixed-versus-growth-mindset/

Fredrickson, B. L. (2001). The role of positive emotions in positive psychology: The broaden-and-build theory of positive emotions. American Psychologist, 56(3), 218–226.

Fredrickson, B. L. (2013). Love 2.0: Finding happiness and health in moments of connection. Penguin.

Fredrickson, B. L., & Joiner, T. (2002). Positive emotions trigger upward spirals toward

emotional well-being. Psychological Science, 13(2), 172–175.

Frijda, N. H. (1986). The Emotions. Cambridge University Press.

Goleman, D. (1995). Emotional intelligence: Why it can matter more than IQ. Bantam Books.

Goleman, D. (2006). Social intelligence: The new science of human relationships. Bantam

Books.

Griffin, J. (1978). A course in miracles. Viking Press.

Hanson, R. (2013). Hardwiring happiness: The new brain science of contentment, calm, and

confidence. Harmony.

Hart, T., Abbott, C., & Chapin, M. (2005). Positive personality changes in acquired brain

injury rehabilitation: The influence of self-transcendence. Rehabilitation Psychology,

50(4), 299-307.

Heckhausen, J., & Schulz, R. (1995). A life-span theory of control. Psychological Review,

102(2), 284-304.

Kabat-Zinn, J. (1990). Full catastrophe living: Using the wisdom of your body and mind to

face stress, pain, and illness. Delta.

Kabat-Zinn, J. (2003). Mindfulness-based interventions in context: Past, present, and future.

Clinical Psychology: Science and Practice, 10(2), 144–156.

Kahneman, D., Diener, E., & Schwarz, N. (Eds.). (1999). Well-being: The foundations of

hedonic psychology. Russell Sage Foundation.

Kashdan, T. B., Biswas-Diener, R., & King, L. A. (2008). Reconsidering happiness: The costs

of distinguishing between hedonics and eudaimonia. Journal of Positive Psychology,

3(4), 219–233.

Kashdan, T. B., & Biswas-Diener, R. (2014). The Upside of Your Dark Side: Why Being Your

Whole Self--Not Just Your "Good" Self--Drives Success and Fulfillment. Hudson Street

Press.

Kasser, T., & Ryan, R. M. (1996). Further examining the American dream: Differential correlates of intrinsic and extrinsic goals. Personality and Social Psychology Bulletin, 22(3), 280–287.

Keyes, C. L. (2007). Promoting and protecting mental health as flourishing: A complementary strategy for improving national mental health. American Psychologist, 62(2), 95–108.

Keyes, C. L. (2009). Atlanta: Flourishing. Journal of Social Issues, 65(4), 853–879.

King, L. A. (2001). The health benefits of writing about life goals. Personality and Social Psychology Bulletin, 27(7), 798-807.

King, L. A. (2016). The science of psychology: An appreciative view. McGraw-Hill Education.

King, L. A., & Hicks, J. A. (2007). Lost and found possible selves, subjective well-being, and ego development in divorced women. Journal of Personality, 75(4), 777–810.

King, L. A., & Napa, C. K. (1998). What makes a life good? Journal of Personality and Social Psychology, 75(1), 156–165.

Kirk, U., Gu, X., Sharp, C., Hula, A., & Fonagy, P. (2013). Mindfulness training increases cooperative decision making in economic exchanges: Evidence from fMRI. Neuroimage, 59(1), 120-127.

Kubzansky, L. D., & Thurston, R. C. (2007). Emotional vitality and incident coronary heart disease: Benefits of healthy psychological functioning. Archives of General Psychiatry, 64(12), 1393–1401.

Langer, E. J. (1989). Mindfulness. Addison-Wesley.

Langer, E. J., Bashner, R., & Chanowitz, B. (1985). Decreasing prejudice by increasing discrimination. Journal of Personality and Social Psychology, 49(5), 113–120.

Langer, E. J., & Moldoveanu, M. (2000). The construct of mindfulness. Journal of Social Issues, 56(1), 1–9.

Leary, M. R. (1983). A brief version of the Fear of Negative Evaluation Scale. Personality and Social Psychology Bulletin, 9(3), 371-375.

Lerner, M. J., & Miller, D. T. (1978). Just world research and the attribution process: Looking back and ahead. Psychological Bulletin, 85(5), 1030–1051.

LePera, N. (2020). How to Do the Work: Recognize Your Patterns, Heal from Your Past, and Create Your Self. Harper Wave.

Lyubomirsky, S. (2007). The how of happiness: A scientific approach to getting the life you want. Penguin.

Lyubomirsky, S., & Layous, K. (2013). How do simple positive activities increase well-being? Current Directions in Psychological Science, 22(1), 57–62.

Lyubomirsky, S., King, L., & Diener, E. (2005). The benefits of frequent positive affect: Does happiness lead to success? Psychological Bulletin, 131(6), 803–855.

Ma, Y., Qin, L., Dong, M., Dong, L., & Liu, Y. (2021). Mindful parenting predicts children's self-regulation via mindful parenting, children's perspective taking, and children's inhibitory control. Mindfulness, 12(1), 160–171.

Maddux, J. E. (2002). Stopping the "madness." In C. R. Snyder & S. J. Lopez (Eds.), Handbook of positive psychology (pp. 5–12). Oxford University Press.

Maddux, J. E. (2005). Self-efficacy: The power of believing you can. In C. R. Snyder & S. J. Lopez (Eds.), Handbook of positive psychology (pp. 277–287). Oxford University Press.

Maslow, A. H. (1943). A theory of human motivation. Psychological Review, 50(4), 370–396.

Maslow, A. H. (1954). Motivation and personality. Harper & Row.

Masten, A. S. (2001). Ordinary magic: Resilience processes in development. American Psychologist, 56(3), 227–238.

McCullough, M. E., Emmons, R. A., & Tsang, J. (2002). The grateful disposition: A conceptual and empirical topography. Journal of Personality and Social Psychology, 82(1), 112–127.

McDougall, W. (1908). An Introduction to Social Psychology. John Barnes.

McDougall, W. (1912). The Disposition of Wishes. Mind, 21(82), 50–63.

McNulty, J. K., & Fincham, F. D. (2011). Beyond positive psychology? Toward a contextual view of psychological processes and well-being. American Psychologist, 67(2), 101–110.

Miao, Z., Mok, I., & Fan, L. (2015). How Chinese Teachers Teach Mathematics And Pursue Professional Development: Perspectives From Contemporary International Research. https://doi.org/10.1142/9789814415828_0002

Mikulincer, M., & Shaver, P. R. (2007). Attachment in adulthood: Structure, dynamics, and change. Guilford Press.

Mikulincer, M., Shaver, P. R., & Pereg, D. (2003). Attachment theory and affect regulation: The dynamics, development, and cognitive consequences of attachment-related strategies. Motivation and Emotion, 27(2), 77–102.

Miller, W. R., & Rollnick, S. (2002). Motivational interviewing: Preparing people for change (2nd ed.). Guilford Press.

Myers, D. G., & Diener, E. (1995). Who is happy? Psychological Science, 6(1), 10–19.

Neenan, M. (2009). Developing resilience: A cognitive-behavioural approach. Routledge.

Norem, J. K. (2001). The positive power of negative thinking. Basic Books.

Norem, J. K., & Chang, E. C. (2002). The positive psychology of negative thinking. Journal of Clinical Psychology, 58(9), 993–1001.

Otake, K., Shimai, S., Tanaka-Matsumi, J., Otsui, K., & Fredrickson, B. L. (2006). Happy people become happier through kindness: A counting kindnesses intervention. Journal of Happiness Studies, 7(3), 361–375.

Pennebaker, J. W. (1997). Writing about emotional experiences as a therapeutic process. Psychological Science, 8(3), 162–166.

Pennebaker, J. W., & Beall, S. K. (1986). Confronting a traumatic event: Toward an understanding of inhibition and disease. Journal of Abnormal Psychology, 95(3), 274–281.

Pennebaker, J. W., & Chung, C. K. (2011). Expressive writing: Connections to physical and mental health. In H. S. Friedman (Ed.), The Oxford handbook of health psychology (pp. 417–437). Oxford University Press.

Pennebaker, J. W., & Seagal, J. D. (1999). Forming a story: The health benefits of narrative.

Journal of Clinical Psychology, 55(10), 1243–1254.

Pennebaker, J. W., & Smyth, J. M. (2016). Opening up by writing it down: How expressive writing improves health and eases emotional pain (3rd ed.). Guilford Press.

Peterson, C., & Seligman, M. E. P. (2004). Character strengths and virtues: A handbook and classification. American Psychological Association and Oxford University Press.

Plomin, R. (2018). Blueprint: How DNA makes us who we are. MIT Press.

Rahmat, N. H. (2018). Educational Psychology: A Tool for Language Research. https://doi.org/10.20319/pijss.2018.42.655668

Ryff, C. D. (1989). Happiness is everything, or is it? Explorations on the meaning of psychological well-being. Journal of Personality and Social Psychology, 57(6), 1069–1081.

Ryff, C. D., & Keyes, C. L. (1995). The structure of psychological well-being revisited. Journal of Personality and Social Psychology, 69(4), 719–727.

Ryan, R. M., & Deci, E. L. (2001). On happiness and human potentials: A review of research on hedonic and eudaimonic well-being. Annual Review of Psychology, 52(1), 141–166.

Ryan, R. M., & Deci, E. L. (2017). Self-Determination Theory: Basic Psychological Needs in Motivation, Development, and Wellness. Guilford Press.

Sapolsky, R. M. (2004). Why zebras don't get ulcers. Owl Books.

Seligman, M. E. P. (1991). Learned optimism. Knopf.

Seligman, M. E. P. (2002). Authentic happiness: Using the new positive psychology to realize your potential for lasting fulfillment. Free Press.

Seligman, M. E. P. (2011). Flourish: A visionary new understanding of happiness and well-being. Free Press.

Seligman, M. E. P., Steen, T. A., Park, N., & Peterson, C. (2005). Positive psychology progress: Empirical validation of interventions. American Psychologist, 60(5), 410–421.

Seligman, M. E. P., Rashid, T., & Parks, A. C. (2006). Positive psychotherapy. American Psychologist, 61(8), 774–788.

Seligman, M. E. P., & Csikszentmihalyi, M. (2000). Positive psychology: An introduction. American Psychologist, 55(1), 5–14.

Sheldon, K. M., & King, L. (2001). Why positive psychology is necessary. American Psychologist, 56(3), 216–217.

Sheldon, K. M., & Lyubomirsky, S. (2006). Achieving sustainable gains in happiness: Change y
our actions, not your circumstances. Journal of Happiness Studies, 7(1), 55–86.

Snyder, C. R., & Lopez, S. J. (Eds.). (2002). Handbook of positive psychology. Oxford University Press.

Snyder, C. R., & Lopez, S. J. (2007). Positive psychology: The scientific and practical explorations of human strengths. Sage Publications.

Snyder, C. R., Sympson, S. C., Ybasco, F. C., Borders, T. F., Babyak, M. A., & Higgins, R. L. (1996). Development and validation of the State Hope Scale. Journal of Personality and Social Psychology, 70(2), 321–335.

Steger, M. F., Oishi, S., & Kashdan, T. B. (2009). Meaning in life across the life span: Levels and correlates of meaning in life from emerging adulthood to older adulthood. The Journal of Positive Psychology, 4(1), 43–52.

Sternberg, R. J. (2003). Wisdom, intelligence, and creativity synthesized. Cambridge University Press.

Stevens, J. (1989). Musicophilia: Tales of music and the brain. Alfred A. Knopf.

Tangney, J. P., Baumeister, R. F., & Boone, A. L. (2004). High self-control predicts good adjustment, less pathology, better grades, and interpersonal success. Journal of Personality, 72(2), 271–324.

Taylor, S. E., & Brown, J. D. (1988). Illusion and well-being: A social psychological perspective on mental health. Psychological Bulletin, 103(2), 193–210.

Taylor, S. E., & Gollwitzer, P. M. (1995). Effects of mindset on positive illusions. Journal of Personality and Social Psychology, 69(2), 213–226.

Taylor, S. E., & Sherman, D. K. (2008). Self-enhancement and self-affirmation: The consequences of positive self-thoughts for motivation and health. In J. Shah & W. L. Gardner (Eds.), Handbook of motivation science (pp. 568–583). Guilford Press.

Taylor, S. E., & Brown, J. D. (1988). Illusion and well-being: A social psychological perspective on mental health. Psychological Bulletin, 103(2), 193–210.

Teasdale, J. D., Segal, Z. V., & Williams, J. M. G. (1995). How does cognitive therapy prevent depressive relapse and why should attentional control (mindfulness) training help? Behaviour Research and Therapy, 33(1), 25–39.

Tedeschi, R. G., & Calhoun, L. G. (2004). Posttraumatic growth: Conceptual foundations and empirical evidence. Psychological Inquiry, 15(1), 1–18.

Tedeschi, R. G., & McNally, R. J. (2011). Can we facilitate posttraumatic growth in combat veterans? American Psychologist, 66(1), 19–24.

Tugade, M. M., & Fredrickson, B. L. (2004). Resilient individuals use positive emotions to bounce back from negative emotional experiences. Journal of Personality and Social Psychology, 86(2), 320–333.

Tugade, M. M., Fredrickson, B. L., & Barrett, L. F. (2004). Psychological resilience and positive emotional granularity: Examining the benefits of positive emotions on coping and health. Journal of Personality, 72(6), 1161–1190.

Unlock Your Full Potential: Proven Meditation Techniques for Strong Me – SIMPLEMENTESOI. HTTPS://SIMPLEMENTESOI.COM/FR/BLOGS/BLOG/UNLOCK-your-full-potential-proven-meditation-techniques-for-strong-mental-health

Vaillant, G. E. (2008). Spiritual evolution: A scientific defense of faith. Broadway Books.

Vaillant, G. E. (2012). Triumphs of Experience: The Men of the Harvard Grant Study. Belknap Press.

Wampold, B. E. (2001). The great psychotherapy debate: Models, methods, and findings. Lawrence Erlbaum Associates.

Waters, L. (2011). A review of school-based positive psychology interventions. The Australian

Educational and Developmental Psychologist, 28(2), 75–90.

Watkins, P. C. (2008). Gratitude and subjective well-being. In M. Eid & R. J. Larsen (Eds.), The science of subjective well-being (pp. 167–192). Guilford Press.

Watkins, P. C., Cruz, L., Holben, H., & Kolts, R. L. (2008). Taking care of business? Grateful processing of unpleasant memories. Journal of Positive Psychology, 3(2), 87–99.

Weiner, B. (1979). A theory of motivation for some classroom experiences. Journal of Educational Psychology, 71(1), 3–25.

Weiner, B. (1986). An attributional theory of motivation and emotion. Springer-Verlag.

Weiner, B. (2000). Intrapersonal and interpersonal theories of motivation from an attributional perspective. Educational Psychology Review, 12(1), 1–14.

Werner, E. E. (1993). Risk, resilience, and recovery: Perspectives from the Kauai longitudinal study. Development and Psychopathology, 5(4), 503–515.

Werner, E. E., & Smith, R. S. (1992). Overcoming the odds: High-risk children from birth to adulthood. Cornell University Press.

Yalom, I. D. (1980). Existential psychotherapy. Basic Books.

Zajonc, R. B. (1980). Feeling and thinking: Preferences need no inferences. American Psychologist, 35(2), 151–175.

ABOUT THE AUTHOR

Maryanne L. Duan is a licensed marriage and family therapist in Orange County, California, and Alaska. While completing her clinical training, Maryanne worked in local government healthcare agencies, where she gained experience helping individuals with severe mental disorders. Maryanne founded All Things Relationship, Inc. in Tustin, CA. All Things Relationship Inc. (AllThingsRelaitonship.org) is a non-profit organization providing psychotherapy and counseling services to meet the specific needs of our clients who encounter difficulties with relationships and marriages, anxiety, depression or other mental illnesses, and challenges of life transitions. All Things Relationship Inc. is also a training site for marriage & family student practicum and associate internship training.

Maryanne lives and enjoys the sunny beaches in Orange County, California, and beautiful nature in Alaska. Reading, arts and crafts, skiing, hiking, foraging, fishing, and music are among her favorite self-care and work-life balance activities.